SIMON &
SCHUSTER

sister

mother

husband

dog

(etc.)

Also by Delia Ephron

Novels

The Lion Is In

Hanging Up

Big City Eyes

Nonfiction & Humor

How to Eat Like a Child

Teenage Romance

Funny Sauce

Do I Have to Say Hello? Aunt Delia's Manners Quiz

Movies
(with Nora Ephron)

You've Got Mail

This Is My Life

Mixed Nuts

Bewitched
(with Nora Ephron, Pete Dexter, and Jim Quinlan)

Michael
(with Elizabeth Chandler)

The Sisterhood of the Traveling Pants

Plays
(with Nora Ephron)

Love, Loss, and What I Wore
(with Judith Kahan and John Forster, music and lyrics)

How to Eat Like a Child

Young Adult

Frannie in Pieces

The Girl with the Mermaid Hair

Children

The Girl Who Changed the World

Santa and Alex

My Life and Nobody Else's

Craft Books
(with Lorraine Bodger)

The Adventurous Crocheter

Gladrags

sister
mother
husband
dog

(etc.)

. . . .

DELIA EPHRON

**SIMON &
SCHUSTER**

London · New York · Sydney · Toronto · New Delhi

A CBS COMPANY

First published in Great Britain by Simon & Schuster UK Ltd, 2013
A CBS COMPANY

Book Design by Amanda Dewey

1 3 5 7 9 10 8 6 4 2

Simon & Schuster UK Ltd
1st Floor
222 Gray's Inn Road
London WC1X 8HB

www.simonandschuster.co.uk

Simon & Schuster Australia, Sydney
Simon & Schuster India, New Delhi

A CIP catalogue record for this book
is available from the British Library

Hardback ISBN: 978-1-47113-185-1
Trade Paperback ISBN: 978-1-47113-244-5
ebook ISBN: 978-1-47113-187-5

Printed and bound by CPI Group (UK) Ltd, Croydon, CR0 4YY

what if a much of a which of a wind

gives the truth to summer's lie;

bloodies with dizzying leaves the sun

and yanks immortal stars awry?

                    e. e. cummings

contents

sister

mother

husband

dog

(etc.)

LOSING NORA

Two weeks after my sister died, I took my dog to the doggie dermatologist. It was a hot day—nearly every day that summer of 2012 was drippingly, tropically humid—and I wasn't sure I should bother to do this because I was exhausted and spacey from loss, but there had been a six-week wait to get an appointment, and, as all my own doctors do, the office had called two days in advance to confirm the appointment. I'd confirmed, so I felt obligated.

Honey was eating her paw. I wasn't sure what paw-eating had to do with dermatology, although my regular vet had suggested it might be connected.

I hadn't been paying much attention to Honey, a small

fluffy white Havanese, except to be grateful for her joyful greetings—yelps that sound like happy weeping and a dash for her squeaky toy gorilla that she paraded around with, waiting for me to applaud, which I did. All my energies had been focused on Nora. But in the middle of one night, I woke up with a start and the realization of what I'd seen but not registered: Honey eating her paw again. Rather obsessively.

Months before, I'd had her paw treated. Actually, I don't know if it was months before—the recent past had managed to wipe out my memory of the less recent past. At some point she'd received a steroid shot from our vet. It hadn't cured her, nor had dipping her paw in some diluted blue liquid.

Until that middle-of-the-night panic attack about Honey, I'd been uncharacteristically calm. Sleeping without assistance (no Tylenol PM or Valium, not even a glass of wine), dropping off to sleep easily, no nightmares or any dreams at all after marathon hours of anxiety in the hospital. This both confused and upset me. If I loved Nora as much as I knew I did, how could I sleep?

Was I aspiring to that fierce will she had, a refusal to show weakness? With Nora, was it more than a refusal? Was it a hatred of weakness, a distaste for it, a pride in not showing it, an unwillingness to give anyone the

satisfaction of seeing it? Perhaps all of those. Nora set
the bar high in the stiff-upper-lip department. Denial
was a talent she greatly admired. She could have been
Gentile, except, of course, she wasn't.

Her point of view about me was that I was a hysteric,
a worrier. Was I trying to disprove her before it was too
late?

When parents die, the dream dies, too—the dream
that they will see you for who you really are (and, I suppose, the dream that they will ever be the parents you
wish for). With sisters is it similar? Did I want Nora to
acknowledge, to realize that I was as tough as she was by
trying to match her, to function on all cylinders and be
absolutely present during this terrifying time?

I had always been amazed at her discipline. I don't
mean as a writer. All four of us sisters—the Ephron
girls, as we were known as children (Nora, Delia, Hallie,
and Amy)—are disciplined. When it comes to writing,
to our careers, we are our mother's daughters: disciplined and driven. But Nora maintained her laser focus
even now, confronting a deadly leukemia. My brain
scrambles when I'm scared, but she could still ask doctors the tough questions and write down the answers in
her graceful, confident penmanship while I could only
scribble unintelligible bits in the corners of paper. (Is

there nothing sisters don't know about each other, nothing they don't compare, even penmanship or note-taking abilities?) Did a tiny piece of me still need to disprove her view of me as a hysteric that I always felt wasn't fair and yet was probably, at least compared to her, accurate?

With sisters, is the competition always marching side by side with devotion? Does it get to be pure love when one of them is dying, or is the beast always hidden somewhere?

Our relationship was so firmly fixed that every day when I went to the hospital I would think, *I'll eat when I get there.* That's what I always thought when we wrote together at her apartment. Nora had a great refrigerator. There was often half a turkey in it or fried chicken in baggies. *Nora will have something for me to eat.* "Sick with cancer and from chemo" was not computing, the odds against her facing death, and still I was expecting to be fed, and usually there were peanut butter and jelly sandwiches that Nick (her husband, Nick Pileggi) had made that she didn't eat and I did.

Everyone involved was steadfast. Everyone was devoted and remarkable. This woman for whom four were better than two, eight better than four, twelve better than six, the more the merrier—this woman for whom entertaining was joy, art, obsession, and religion—was reduced to the same small rotating cast all struggling to make her happy, all praying (except none of us pray) for healthy white blood cells to sprout, for the marrow to be fertile.

Nora thanked me by sending me roses—two dozen gorgeous plump peach roses in full bloom—the sister in the hospital sending flowers to the one who was not.

I have thought a lot about this. More than anything, I think about this.

There are things a person does that you could talk about forever. They are the key. They reveal character, they unlock secrets. I think Nora's sending me flowers was that.

It meant flat out *I love you*. Did the note say that? I'm not sure. I think it was simply, *Love, Nora*. It could have been, *xx, Nora*. My blanks in memory even include important emotional things like that. It also meant *thank you*, obviously. She was grateful for my presence, although gratitude was . . . Well, my presence wasn't anything I needed to be thanked for. It was hard to be away from her. Leaving felt like abandonment. It felt obscene that I could leave that place and she could not. It seemed impossible. It felt dangerous to leave.

Being there was an imperative. There was no way to be anyplace else.

Nora's sending me roses . . . not only painfully sweet, but how difficult it must have been for her to be needing care, to be dependent, vulnerable. A tiny difficult, a tiny horrible compared to the trapdoor about to open, but still not a place she was comfortable.

Don't misunderstand. All I'm saying is those roses had subtext. A heartbreaking way to have a bit of control. To get to the place where she "lived." The driver, not the passenger. Those roses were all that in addition to being a gift of love.

Nora was brilliant at giving. Something was always arriving by messenger. Ginger cookies she brought back from San Francisco. Peanut butter cookies from Seattle. Chocolate marshmallow drops. She would call: "These are amazing. I'm sending some down to you this very second."

Last Christmas she gave us down jackets that my husband, Jerry, and I lived in. I not only wore mine outside all winter, but often in the kitchen when I was cooking because it was so light and warm at the same time. Once I came home from a birthday dinner. I hadn't had any cake, and I love cake. As I walked into the lobby of my building, I thought, *Nora will have sent me a cake*, and the doorman said, "I have a package for you." It was my favorite, the yellow cake with pink frosting from Amy's Bread.

So brilliant at giving. At receiving, not so much. After years of hunting in vain for something she would like for Christmas or her birthday, I pretty much picked the first possibility and let go of the impossible, that I might please her. Occasionally she might anoint something randomly. Her sporadic, unpredictable seal of approval was brilliant power-wise—power was something she had an innate understanding of—because it could keep a person hoping. A friend of hers mentioned to me with considerable pride that Nora liked her brisket.

Once I gave Nora a backpack purse. A week later I went to the store and bought one for myself. I was pretty sure that the purse I purchased was the very one I'd given her (that she'd brought back). When I wore it to her house a few weeks later, she said, "I love that, I want one." I said, "Get real. I gave it to you, and you returned it."

The same thing happened in the hospital.

She sent me to a store that specializes in hats for women who have had chemotherapy.

I hated that Nora was losing her hair. Even mentioning it feels like a betrayal. Her hair was gorgeous and thick and always looked fabulous. I know, the deal is to be proud, to face the world bald. It is heartbreaking to lose your hair, though compared with dying, not so much. I get it. But what about no hair *and* dying?

I hate the nickname "chemo." I like to nickname only people or things I love. My dog has about twenty-two nicknames. My husband, at least seven. I suppose some patients want to think of chemotherapy as their friend, an ally, hence a nickname, but chemotherapy is way too cruel for a nickname. In Nora's case, chemotherapy was more likely either not going to work or to kill rather than save. Calling chemotherapy "chemo" is like calling napalm "nappy." Until the effects of Nora's chemotherapy kicked in, volunteers (sweet teenaged girls who used to be called candy stripers) would show up every day and, in a sort of inept Mitt Romney-ish way, start a conversation by guessing at our relationship. "Are you sisters?" "Are you twins?" Twelve or so days into chemotherapy, a volunteer walked into the room, looked at Nora and then at me, and said to me, "Is she your mother?"

Twelve days on chemotherapy and my sister often mistaken for my twin is mistaken for my mother. That's chemotherapy.

On her instructions, I went to the store for a particular hat. A soft three-cornered sort of cap, she told me, or
words to that effect. One style seemed most likely what
she meant, although perhaps not, so I bought everything.
Every style they had.

All wrong, she told me. Every one.

Should I throw them away? I asked. (The store did
not allow returns.)

Nora told me to toss the one I thought came closest
and put the rest on the shelf. A few days later, she sent
someone else for the three-cornered cap, and that person
came back with the very same thing I did. She showed it
to me. "Look, this is what I wanted."

"That's exactly what I gave you," I said, and began
frantically looking for it, couldn't find it, and then
vaguely remembered she'd told me to toss it. This had
taken place only a few days earlier, but my brain was
fogged. The experience was like a dream. I couldn't be
sure it happened. Really, Nora could be a total frus-
tration, as hard to please now as ever. She was the same
person, only a very sick same person, and I was grateful for that crankiness because it meant she was still
there, but really all I wanted to do was to get in bed
with her. I wanted to get under the covers and lie next
to her. I tried it, too, but there wasn't really room. She

had so many tubes. Why don't they have double beds in hospitals?

If I had a hospital, I'd have double beds in it.

. . . .

Being in a hospital sucks. It sucks worse if you're poor and not famous, because at least if you're rich and famous you can afford a private room, and depending on your course of treatment reside on the fancy floor with a view of the river. (For most of Nora's illness, because of the chemotherapy she was receiving, she could not stay there.) And the hospital cares. A lovely woman from patient services arrives to ask if everything is okay. Hospitals need rich people, because they are going broke. They need famous people, because lots of people want to be in the same hospital a famous person went to. Hospitals need their beds filled. Besides, no one wants anything to happen to a national treasure on his watch. And Nora was/is a national treasure.

(Verb tense has begun to confuse me. I have three sisters, I had three sisters. I have two sisters. I have three sisters. Nora is a national treasure.)

So here we are, not leaving her alone for a second in

case something goes wrong, but we have no idea what could go wrong. One morning we don't notice that some pills that she didn't take are sitting on the table. What do I mean, we don't notice? We don't notice because we don't know we're supposed to be looking there for that. A relatively minor mistake (although is there such a thing when a person is this sick?), but how can we possibly know all the ins and outs of the protocol of this particular chemotherapy, and besides, there are the heart meds because her heart might get wonky on the chemotherapy, and so forth and so on.

All the various specialists come in, doing their dance. There are many ramifications of this treatment, potential disasters galore. Glitches happen every day, and we have no idea what the glitch is, what it even could be. It's not as if there's a sniper in the woods and everyone keeps their eyes on the trees, searching for a man with a gun. No one knows where the hell they should be looking or what the hell they should be looking for until something starts beeping. Or maybe there will be no beep and we don't know to expect one.

I felt a pervasive sense of helplessness. Of danger. Of responsibility. And a pervasive sense of guilt and unreality. How could she be sick and not me?

. . . .

She was born first. Solo. I was born a sister. Three years younger. I can only imagine her horror when I turned up. It was the first thing in her life that she had no control over.

So many women have come up to me, telling me she was their role model, and she was mine, too. I used to joke that I ran for the same class offices she did and lost as she did. Looking back, that's a loaded comment, isn't it? I mean, it doesn't take a shrink. I wasn't going to best her, upset the balance of power, my place in the world. It didn't cross my mind until I was out of college that my job as a younger sister was not to imitate but to differentiate.

But how? We are sisters, collaborators, writer-children of writer-parents who collaborated. How am I not her? How did I find my way when she took up so much space?

It's probably a fair generalization that famous people take up more space than people who are not famous. (They are not the only ones. Difficult children take up more space than children who are easy. Addict personalities pull focus.) People with big talent and big fame suck more oxygen out of a room. Partly it's their nature, and partly it's the excitement that other people feel in their presence. Those of us who grow up around it or live in proximity have to deal with it.

My writing *How to Eat Like a Child*—five hundred words about children and food that appeared in the *New York Times Magazine*—was my first big success and the first time I understood my own voice, truly heard it. I was thirty-two. I remember the sudden awareness and surprise. *Oh, this is who I am.* Our job as writers, as we begin that journey, is to figure out what we can do. Only do what you can do. It's a rule I live by. Among other things, it means I can have novels heavier with dialogue than description. But more important, if you only do what you can do, you never have to worry that someone else is doing it. It keeps you from competing. It keeps you looking inside for what's true rather than outside for what's popular. Ideally. Your writing is your fingerprint.

It's our job in life to come to some understanding of our own identity, and being a writer makes that easier. *What do I think? What do I love? What do I see? What are my stories?* come up over and over again and/or reveal themselves, sometimes unintentionally, over and over again.

At Nora's memorial service, Martin Short quoted Nora: "Hazelnuts are what's wrong with Europe." It got a big laugh. It was my line. Tom Hanks quoted this dialogue about falling in love from *Sleepless in Seattle*: "It was like coming home, but not to any home I'd ever known." Also mine—from my wedding. I'd popped it into the script. (It turns out, even though you never wear a wedding dress twice, you can recycle your vows.) Some weeks later, Frank Rich in *New York* magazine quoted another line of Nora's: "Never marry a man you wouldn't want to be divorced from."

"That's mine," I said to my husband. I looked in one of her collections. There it was. I tried to recall if she asked permission to use it. I don't remember. I've probably used hers. For all I know, I'm going to do it in the next paragraph. Our words and thoughts are muddied together in life and in the movies we collaborated on. We borrowed lines from each other the way other sisters borrow dresses.

I spent my life turning all my girlfriends into sisters; perhaps easier, more relaxed versions of my relationships with my sisters, surely warmer, more supportive versions of my mother. I confided more safely and intimately in my closest girlfriends. When my husband got cancer (now in remission), Nora and I rarely discussed it. Isn't that odd? I couldn't, because I was always trying to prove my bravery, and she didn't ask, perhaps respecting my privacy, perhaps relieved not to know. I have no idea. It's one of those weird things that make no sense. How could we be so devoted and not talk about the most earth-shattering thing in my life? But sister relationships are quirky, all family relationships are. Some things are proof of nothing, and some are proof of everything.

This is complicated, trying to understand how we were close. Losing her is like losing an arm, it's that de-ranging. But in regard to the daily pains of my life, the fears, the anxieties, the worries, I relied on my husband and my friends. Nora didn't have the patience I needed. She didn't allow herself any moping or self-pity. I like a good mope now and then.

That is one way we are different. One way we were different.

When I read the heapings of love from every corner after she died, I did wonder if she was cozier with a few of those who were her friends than with me, the way I am cozier with my husband and with my best friends. Certainly the need to claim a relationship/ownership after her death was awesome. One writer trashed other wonderful loving tributes, jockeying for position, as if to say, *Forget those guys, I was the one she really loved.*

Was I surprised by how many people wanted to claim they were in her inner circle? She was generous to so many, but how could they have been close to her if they knew nothing really? If they could all look back at their relationship, at the six years she'd been ill, like a cheated-upon spouse and had to reevaluate every encounter in light of new information? Maybe that's what fueled it (all that claiming), that confusion. They were in the inner circle and they were not. Both are true. Some things are proof of nothing and some are proof of everything.

As busloads of strangers tell me what she meant to them, I sympathize with Caroline Kennedy. This is ridiculous, me and Caroline, I know, I know, we have nothing in common, and yet I do think about her, because losing her daddy has nothing to do with millions of Americans losing a president. Yet how many people must have come up to her with the need to share that they entered the Peace Corps because of him, or were driving down the Taconic when they heard he was shot, burst into tears, and had to pull over, or that their dad worshipped the ground he walked on, now *that* was a president.

In my case, what I remember most about Kennedy dying (I was a freshman in college and obviously an idiot, read on) is debating with my friends whether it was disrespectful to make out on the weekend after the president had been assassinated, which is not something I would ever mention to Caroline if the opportunity arose. Anyway, when that need to share finally subsided, which was maybe decades, and Caroline could finally leave the house without meeting someone who named their cat JFK, her mother died, and everyone was telling her how much they admired Jackie, how brave she was, how they bought the same striped calypso tees . . . only Caroline had lost her mother, not a national widow or a style icon. Then, just as that was over (although it might not yet be), her brother John's airplane crashed . . .

She has spent her life consoling other people for her loss.

She has also spent her life being reminded of her loss daily by caring people who don't know her but who offer their condolences because it is the proper thing to do and because it is their loss, too, but without considering that the loss is entirely different and without considering that it might not be as easy for her to accept their sympathies as it is for them to give them. It might, for instance, evoke pain. It often blindsides me.

It also brings death into the day, and at this age death feels like it's a car's length behind, anyway. It's best to be in the moment. It's always best to be in the moment. At one event where I was speaking—a version of this happens often—a woman went into gales of laughter about how when she put on a turtleneck that morning she

thought of Nora. A stranger visiting someone in my apartment building rang my doorbell to tell me that he had
been with my sister "in group." (This would be group
therapy—about forty years ago.) People share their ill-
nesses and their losses, people whose names I often don't
know, *Hi, I just want you to know I have cancer, too*, or
my sister did, or *I just lost my sister* or *my mother* or *my
brother.* I don't know what to do with all the sadness.

There is so much artificial intimacy these days, it's
not surprising there is postmortem intimacy. The ubiquitous Facebook—full of real friends and fake friends. All
that thumbs up—it's as if one is living in a virtual cheering squad. The other day I was scrolling through the
News Feed and came upon a close-up of someone's mother
waking up after surgery. Did her mother have any idea
she had been snapped and posted? She was barely con-
scious. The violation was shocking. When my dog Honey
was hit by a car, I posted it on Facebook and found the
messages heartening. With Nora, I don't. I can't process
it.

The love and fun of Nora is now replaced by the leg-
acy of Nora. What she means to others and to me (and
to her children, her husband, my sisters, etc.) is entirely
different. The Nor and Del (pronounced *Deal*) of it. The
Hi, it's me, call me. The intimacy that wasn't the intimacy

of *I'll tell you what I'm really feeling*, but was the intimacy of *I'll open your refrigerator and take whatever I want*.

Our lives were in some ways entirely separate and unknown to each other, in other ways like vines twisted together. Invading her privacy is not something I want to do. Where that line is, is subjective. Perhaps to you I have already crossed it or I will cross it, but to me I have not and will not. During the years she was sick, we talked often about her illness. The conversations were easy only in the sense that we felt safe together and could speak intimately, but they are painful to recall and will always be secret and sacred. Some things can be told and some cannot.

Why am I writing about her/us at all? Because writing is how I understand everything that happens. Writing is the only way I know to move on.

Also, it's comforting to go into my office at four every afternoon and write about us. It's the only thing that really is, actually. A way to be together.

Last winter, when I gave a speech in Seattle, they told me that when Nora had been there a couple of years before, she had told them that the dressing room smelled moldy and they should fix it. So they renovated it. Nora told the managers of the theater where our play *Love,*

Loss, and What I Wore was performed that they needed better toilet paper. "Our audience needs decent toilet paper," she said. Recently I told the Marriott Hotel in Miami that they shouldn't have cocktail napkins at their breakfast buffet, they should have big cloth napkins. I told Craftbar, a restaurant I frequent, that they simply could not be open for brunch and not have the biscuits ready. It was unacceptable.

Is this misplaced anger at the unfairness of her death? Is that why I have spent the short time that has since passed irritated—well, more accurately, walking around in a simmering, smoldering rage? The anger feels great. Life-affirming. Far preferable to the pain it's masking.

With my newly found aggression, am I carrying on her tradition? Is it the middle child rises? I know—these forays into bossiness are feeble compared to Nora's, but I'm just getting started. One of her gifts was to set the record straight, help all of us live our lives. Does wallpaper belong in the front hall? What kind of stuffing does the couch need? When I first started writing, she told me, "Always know what you think." Oh my God, who always knows what they think (although it's important when you write, it's true)? She did. I thought she left me enough guidance for several lives, but today I ate a kale salad. Kale is everywhere. And panko. What did she think of kale and panko?

It's a whole new world in an awful and confusing way. A city in which the street signs are missing.

Perhaps that's why I am losing things and spend a lot of time every day racing from one room to another trying to find my glasses/phone/keys/whatever I put down a second earlier. (I wish someone would invent a way to phone your keys.) I can't stop for grief, which is surely why I am irritated. Life is too short, my motor is racing, and I want only to move forward. This is what dogs do and why they seem a model for living well. They are always in the moment.

. . . .

Nora was powerful. In a room full of people, heads turned her way. Would she approve? Everyone wanted to please her. Were they smart enough? Funny enough? Personally I believe she was genius at giving and withholding at the same time, a potent combination, but that's just what I think.

She was also ruthless as a writer. Shortly after her death, I was at a panel where two actors each read a piece of hers. In one, Nora shoved a dagger into Alix Kates

Shulman for writing about how difficult it is to be beautiful. In another she nailed a relative. And all anyone on the panel mentioned was how sweet Nora was, how witty, how generous, and what an extraordinary craftsman. No one mentioned the daggers. Or her take-no-prisoners toughness, her "I will throw you under the bus for a good story" (something she admitted to). Intolerance of what she viewed as stupidity was the talent and terror of her.

Talent makes its own demands. Big talent is a force with a mind of its own, except it is *your* mind. A gift is a pulsing creature, almost in a sci-fi way, needing to burst out. She had no choice but to let it loose. It was great security to know that, needing me as much as I needed her, Nora wouldn't turn her unsparing eye on me. I once turned mine on her, however, sending her up when I created Georgia, a wildly opinionated, wildly successful, self-centered older sister in my novel *Hanging Up.* I thanked Nora for not getting upset about it. "But she was such a great character," she said.

Nora always said that we shared half a brain. The knowledge of how similar we were, how much we appreciated each other, depended on each other, made each other laugh, could live without many other people but not without each other, was solace and joy for both of us.

But she needed to be on top. She needed to travel

around the track faster than anyone, not just me. When I was younger, I fancied or joked that she was moving so fast because she knew I was on her tail, but really she was simply a Thoroughbred, born and bred to race and win. She was the filly who won the Kentucky Derby. (And there have only been three: Regret [1915], Genuine Risk [1980], and Winning Colors [1988].)

In *Little Women*, the novel by Louisa May Alcott about four sisters, which was a seminal book for me in my childhood, Beth, the third sister, dies. I was obsessed with Beth. I compulsively searched that novel to find the exact place where Beth dies, where it says Beth dies or what she died of. She slipped into the valley of shadow, a frustrating vagueness like that. It didn't satisfy me. I needed to know.

I identified with Beth, which makes no sense because Beth was third of four and I was second of four. Technically I was Jo. Possibly I became Beth in my head because Nora was so obviously Jo, the one with ambition. Although Jo was a tomboy and a rebel, as was I, and Nora was not. Perhaps the death of my uncle in his thirties, to some sort of cancer never explained, when I was a child accounts for my obsession with death. I remember being at Camp Tocaloma, a sleepaway camp I hated that my mother sent us to every August. I remember wishing on a star, wishing every night, that Uncle Dickie would live, but he did not.

I also remember being on the playground and realizing that, if I was eight, I had lived eight years. Before that, in my child's understanding, I had lived forever and was called eight. That actual time was involved, eight years, struck me with terror. Life/death. Finite. Not forever. I would die.

All my life that fear, *I will die, I will cease to exist*, has haunted me. That thing—when you're dead, you don't know it—really got me as a kid and stuck. And here it was, death, but not mine, Nora's.

. . . .

Nora and I wrote a pilot when she was in the hospital.

Before the debilitating effects of chemotherapy would kick in, there was an eight-day window (maybe nine, maybe seven, maybe ten, maybe twelve. Don't expect factual accuracy here, I would flunk that test. Everything from that time is cloudy). Nora mentioned that she recently had had a meeting about a pilot for cable TV. An hour-long pilot is only forty pages, she said, we can write it in a weekend. Perhaps it was fifty pages, she wasn't sure, we'd have to check on that. Still, we could write it.

Of course, I said. What is it?

It was about an SEC officer (woman) and a CEO of an investment bank (man). Staggeringly rich, he's corrupt in the way many/all bank CEOs in this world seem to be, imagining they're not, doing tricky things we don't know about, disdaining us for not understanding things they often don't understand themselves. She (the SEC officer), a middle-class woman from Queens, gets assigned to his bank to police him.

Explain selling short to me again? I said, testing out my ability to wrap my brain around a Wall Street story. She did. I failed to grasp it, as usual. She was the one with the math brain. (Amy and Hallie have math brains, too, and if you want to know who has the best hands of the four of us, it's me.) Anyway, I knew a bit about banks. I have a savings and a checking account. Nora mentioned Dodd-Frank (a federal law intended to police bank behavior). She could handle Dodd-Frank. One of the great things about collaboration is you don't need to know everything yourself, you need to know everything between the two of you. Frankly I don't think she had a clue about Dodd-Frank, either. But this was a pilot. We didn't need to understand Dodd-Frank until episode three. We weren't thinking about episode three.

We were hoping only to get her through chemo-therapy.

George and Martha, as we called the pilot, was an alternate universe. A place for her to live.

We did write it in a weekend. Then we rewrote it. Sometimes I would arrive in the morning and find changes. She'd worked at night after I'd left.

We worked on her laptop at a circular table in the room, outlining first, the way we always did, jotting ideas for characters. Taking turns at the computer as we always did. We discussed lunch, something we always loved to do, but the choices were more limited—tuna sandwiches on whole wheat (not too much tuna—we didn't like fat sandwiches) or ham and cheese on whole wheat from the deli two blocks away, or soup from Au Bon Pain in the lobby of the hospital.

We gave the script to the producer, Scott Rudin. He read it within a day or two. This promptness was unusual in my experience, especially since he had no idea that, as they say regarding movie plot gimmicks, there was a ticking clock.

We were going to have a notes meeting. This was all in the context of the secrecy of Nora's illness. Like many people, Rudin knew that Nora was in the hospital, but not that her situation was serious.

Dragging the chemotherapy drip to which she was tethered twenty-four hours a day (but was soon to be un-tethered from, making the meeting possible), Nora and I scouted the café on the fourth floor as a potential loca-tion. It was quite pretty—modern, blond wood. I think there was a waterfall. (Perhaps I've invented the waterfall. Waterfalls are soothing and peaceful—the hospital should install one if it isn't there already.) This briefest of treks was almost jaunty. Not at all, of course, and yet . . . we'd scouted locations together before. Some joy of past ad-ventures, a familiar fun way of being together, buoyed us the tiniest bit. (I wonder if I've imagined this in re-trospect, this uptick in mood lasting maybe ten min-utes. I'd hate to be romanticizing even a second of this awfulness.) In the end we did the notes meeting on the phone: Nora in bed, me in the chair, the cell phone on speaker lying on the sheet between us like another pa-tient, an itty bitty one.

She got into a disagreement about the ending. She was weakened by this time, and the heart monitor started beeping, too. It was a madness. She dug in her heels—would Martha be assigned to the bank at the end of epi-sode one? Nora would not agree to it . . . in her way, not arguing, simply refusing to accede. They hit a bit of an impasse. I was thinking, *Who cares?* But of course you have to care, because if you don't, it's the end. Right? I guess. I don't really know. If you were an actor playing Nora, arguing about something that inconsequential, that would be the subtext, you have to keep caring or you're dead, that would layer it with meaning. Perhaps in life it was what it was: simply in character. Or a blessed minute of normalcy.

One day I was writing a scene, it was about four o'clock, which is when I always need a latte. I was at the computer. She was in bed. Truly, I was groggy with exhaustion. "I can't write this scene, I'm too tired," I said.

"Yes, you can," she said.

I did. It wasn't a bad scene. She liked it. "Oh, this is good." I loved getting compliments from her. I loved it so much, I often didn't show her things to free me of the need.

This collaboration was only a small part of what life was. This alternate universe. All of us caring for her were living in an alternate universe, as was she. The pilot made it a double alternate. An alternate alternate. Beyond beyond. Anyone who is in the hospital or trying to care for someone in a hospital knows how real life evaporates.

One day Jamie Dimon, CEO of JPMorgan Chase, was

going to testify before something like Congress—it would be on C-SPAN. "We should watch," said Nora. But we didn't.

That's the last I remember of us and *George and Martha*. The cancer or the chemotherapy or a combination of both now had the upper hand.

I was scrolling through e-mails to find out when that was. How far from the end? E-mails might give me a hint because it was our habit to e-mail the script at the end of the day. If we were at her apartment, we e-mailed it to me, and vice versa. We had continued to do this, although less regularly, at the hospital. I was unable to pinpoint the date (my guess is about ten days before she died). Instead I found, from the end of January through April, a slew of e-mails about my living room couch. "My couch is dowdy," I'd written her. She reassured me that I could probably fix it by getting it more stuffed. I had made a huge mistake, I wrote back, re-covering it in a hideous fabric—a mistake as bad as the pumpkin-colored Fiat I'd once purchased and a West End Avenue apartment (that was my worst mistake), all dramas she'd lived through. We had sat on the floor of that empty apartment trying to figure out if I really could live there. I couldn't.

In spite of all our anxiety about her health during those months—frequent talks and updates on the telephone—our sisterhood was continuing online at its most normal, with us sending pictures of possible replacement couches back and forth. At one point she e-mailed me from a couch store, urging me to hop in a taxi and come over, she thought she'd found one. I wrote her asking/bemoaning, *What's wrong with my living room?* After double-checking to make sure I wanted to hear, she dove in. She actually thought my couch was fine, but I needed new lamps, my chairs would be better off in the bedroom, and it was possible my coffee table was making too much of a statement. She offered to meet me at Mecox Gardens, a shop on Lexington Avenue, for lamps.

When I came upon all these couch exchanges, I remembered that one particularly, the one where she had dissected my living room, but I couldn't find it. It was gone. It's as if it deleted itself and all that is left are the sweetest—twenty in all.

. . . .

I had learned Nora was sick six years earlier. I'd come home from Paris—my husband and I had been there for New Year's Eve, and it had been the best New Year's Eve of my life. We'd rented an apartment, and many of our close friends were there, and we'd had a fantastic party. When I came home there was a message from Nora: "Are you back yet?"

She'd waited until I got home before bothering me with the news that she was not only sick, but the doctors thought she had six months to live. Jerry and I went up to her apartment. All I remember from that night was fear. It was in the room the way air was. We were all terrified. And that she showed me her hand. It was as white as marble.

I find myself often looking at my own hand, turning the palm up, taking some weird survivor relief that it is pinkish. Waiting for the day when it is not.

Nora was terminally ill. It was as if the Earth had shifted on its axis, something unfathomable had occurred in the galaxy in which I lived.

Sometime after knowing about her illness but before she was stabilized on treatment—when, I'm not exactly sure—I was walking down a Greenwich Village street thinking desperately, truly desperately, *I need something from her, I need something.* A few days later we were working at my apartment on our play, *Love, Loss, and What I Wore.* I was sitting at the computer, and she was behind me and she said, "I have this ring that you should have. It's a pansy ring, and you love pansies." Which I do, they are my favorite flower (and one of Honey's middle names). She took off the ring and gave it to me.

And the end of that story should be, *And I never took the ring off.* But I did, because that enamel pansy got caught on things, and several times it practically yanked my finger off. I often took the ring off, and one day I lost it. My guess is it fell off the bedside table and my dog ate it (and perhaps that is why she is eating her paw), but why would she? More likely the vacuum cleaner sucked it up.

I drove myself crazy trying to find it. I can't bear that it's gone.

. . . .

I have been wondering whether Nora's refusal to reveal her illness, her decision to keep it a secret, is something people will aspire to the way they followed her advice about egg white omelets. To those people, I want to say that she wasn't always right. Five years ago, she told me to sell my Apple stock.

Not telling was the right choice because it was the one she wanted to make. It was her illness and her death, hers and nobody else's. Whether you want to let others in on your battle with a life-threatening disease isn't how you want to die, it's how you want to live.

I have been astonished that some people have criticized it, that they think they have any right to judge. Christopher Hitchens, the writer who chronicled his battle with cancer in article after article, chose to examine his illness minutely, letting everyone in on the pain, the medicine, the madness, and the endgame. Robin Roberts of ABC's *Good Morning America*, who had a bone marrow transplant, took viewers along with her, inviting cameras into her hospital room, demystifying, erasing stigma, dramatically increasing the number of bone marrow donors. They are both heroes to me, as is my sister. There is no right way. We're talking about death. It's okay to be scared witless. I say that because it might be my way.

Secrets are tricky, no question about it. They can eat away at you, especially if they involve guilt or shame. Mostly no one can keep them. Ben Franklin said the only way three people can keep a secret is if two of them are dead. (Maybe Ben's sister said that and Ben borrowed it.) Secret-keeping where illness is concerned requires an ability to mask. Not everyone can do that. Gossip is ugly when it's mean-spirited or gleeful about someone else's catastrophe. But sometimes gossip isn't gossip, it's only sharing, a way to understand, make sense of life, lessen confusion, dissipate fear.

In the case of my sister, there were a host of considerations. Her movie career might have been compromised. Would actors commit? Would the studio allow it? You can direct if you are known to be sick, but you need another director to agree to finish the film just in case (which is what Robert Altman had arranged before he died). If you are famous and you are sick and you tell, you become a famous sick person. You can't draw a line. If you're out there with it, everyone, I mean *everyone*, knows it. And because they have read your books or seen your movies and loved or identified with them/you, people on the street feel familiar enough to offer comfort, confide their own traumas, pray for you (which is not something most atheists crave) when, despite good intentions, what they're also doing is reminding you that you are sick. Also, Nora loved fun, and if friends knew she was sick, that might get in the way of it—in the way of their fun for sure, hers too depending on how well denial was working.

Telling is also a loss of control. Of power. The person with the secret is the person with the power. (Remember the roses.)

Nora told many people she loved them during the last months of her life, but without letting them know why she suddenly went mushy. I think having people cry over her would have been too much. That's just a guess.

(Again those roses.)

Many people, some whom I know, some curious strangers, ask me if we debated telling. And some writers have insinuated that she had an obligation to the living. They were poleaxed. How dare she?

If I had said to Nora, which I wouldn't have because it was not the point and unfair besides, but if I had said, "So-and-so will be upset not to know," I like to think she might have said, "I'll be dead." I like to think she'd say it because she always knew to call a spade a spade. Meaning *It's not my problem*, but much more to the point, *I'm the one who is dying. I'm the one who is fucked. They have the luxury of being upset about it.* That doesn't mean she didn't love everyone. Of course her children did know, and a few others who were very close, but everyone else will survive.

When she entered the hospital we almost did release the information, but then changed our minds. In retrospect, it seems the right choice, because the news coverage would have overwhelmed/distressed her, all of us, and diverted energy and focus. But we didn't expect her to die in five weeks. We hoped she would live—we all hoped she would live to see *Lucky Guy* on Broadway starring Tom Hanks, and if she didn't go into remission that she would limp along for a while, maybe go home and we would deal with the problem then.

I'm glad she didn't tell, because one of the things I admired the most about her was her refusal to go down. To let "them" see her pain. To let people feel bad for her.

. . . .

Critics were hard on her, much harder than on male directors who did half as good work. This country likes to take down strong women. Everyone loved Hillary more after Bill cheated during his presidency. In her own campaign for president, her popularity spiked when she cried during the run-up to the New Hampshire primary. Martha Stewart was sent to jail to jeers of satisfaction. Michelle Obama, who could mow us all down with her intelligence, pretends to be all about motherhood. Defang the women: It's a national pastime in which women are both the victims and collaborators.

Nora, in the most irritating way (to many people), came back from stuff. Carl Bernstein (her first husband) betrayed her when she was seven months pregnant. She wrote a bestseller about it, *Heartburn*, which became a movie. Then she fell in love with Nick and married happily ever after. *Lucky Numbers*, a black comedy, and *Bewitched* put her in movie jail (what they call a director whom no one wants to hire). She wrote herself out of it with *Julie & Julia*. *Imaginary Friends*, an inventive and playful play, was insanely trashed. Even check out the reviews for the film we wrote together, *You've Got Mail*, which is beloved: begrudging. So regarding the outpouring of affection . . . because I am my sister's sister, and my mother's daughter, I have to point out the obvious. How easy for everyone now. Nora finally did something she can't bounce back from. She died.

Nora and I were not huggers. We never greeted each other that way or often even with a kiss on the cheek. One day, when we left a doctor's appointment—one of the first appointments about the thing we had been dreading for six years, that her disease had morphed into something dreadful—when we left that appointment at the hospital and walked along the curving driveway to the street, I linked my arm in hers. It was the first time in our lives that I had ever done so.

. . . .

Somewhere in there, in the midst of the intense chaos that followed, the daily worries, the vigil, the relentless caring and helplessness that had overtaken our lives, I realized my dog was chewing her paw and got a recommendation from my vet for a specialist. Here it was weeks later, Nora was dead, and Honey had a two o'clock appointment.

I was thinking about how Nora liked corn flakes while the vet took Honey's history. When did her paw-chewing first start? Was it worse in certain seasons? Was it only one paw, was it occasionally other paws? Was she drinking more water?

I tried to focus. I couldn't activate a search. "Does everyone know the answer to these?"

"Yes," she said.

"I don't." I considered whether to mention my sister had died. How perfect. Nora never admitted her fatal disease, no excuse she shows up, and I am a second from blaming my bad dog-mothering on her.

The vet rattled on—did I want to rule out a bacterial infection versus a yeast infection (yeast being worse) for a hundred and twenty-five dollars more? I said yes— how could I not? The bliss of being a dog, of not knowing what you are in for, became abundantly clear as Honey, not realizing she was going for an unpleasant medical procedure, went happily into the elevator with the doctor.

While I waited, I hung out with Nora. I don't mean I sensed her presence. I wish I had. She's simply part of my consciousness, more or less lurking. I remembered Nora's telling me she was good at tree pose. Tree pose is a yoga position.

Nora came very late to yoga, and when she told me she did it I found it hard to imagine. She didn't like to do anything she couldn't spin into multitasking. Nora looked so cute doing tree pose. To hold your balance, you have to focus on a point in the distance, some point, just fix on it, balance on one leg and bend the other so that your foot rests on your calf or thigh. Tree pose requires discipline, a quality she liked, as opposed to *shavasana*, that thing at the end of a yoga session where you lie on the floor and vegetate. I imagine Nora would have said, "Let's skip that."

The dermatologist returned. "Good news. Honey does not have a yeast infection. She has to go on a kangaroo diet."

"What?"

"She has a food allergy, that's the likely explanation, and she has to eat kangaroo."

They make kangaroo into dog food? I don't know what to say. You can eat kangaroo? Is that legal? I have to call Nora. Honey has to eat kangaroo.

Nora would love it. Or would she have loved it? Would she have been reading her e-mails while she talked to me? Would I have had a sudden sense that no one was at the other end of the line? She wasn't really interested in dogs, while I could talk about dogs for the rest of my life. Still, usually when the conversation turns to dogs, you know the party is five minutes from being over.

When the conversation turns to dogs, you know the party is five minutes from being over. Maybe Nora would have borrowed that line. Well, she won't be doing that anymore, will she?

. . . .

Now it's fall and Honey no longer chews her paw. The doctor cured her. Sun Golds, the most perfect tomatoes in the world, are finished for the season and no longer for sale in the Union Square Greenmarket. Pumpkins are everywhere. It's cool out. I'm wearing my leather jacket.

Once I mentioned to Nora that I wanted all my personal papers destroyed when I died, and she agreed in words to this effect—I am not quoting exactly, although I know her voice well enough to make it sound that way: "What is there left to say? I've said everything."

Not hardly. Articles about her are continuing to pop

up everywhere, often with yet another adorable photo I've never seen before. I've begun to wonder if she is going to become the Jewish Marilyn Monroe.

W. H. Auden, who understands everything about the human condition, begins a poem about the loss of his lover with "Stop all the clocks."

Yes, stop them for the people I love. For my sister. It would be the decent thing to do.

But the clocks keep ticking, insulting our grief, forcing us into new realities, cheering us up, making us laugh, taunting us with the possibility of forgetting, zapping us with the pain of remembering.

It was a privilege to see her out. Perhaps it's obvious that being there is a privilege when you love someone, but I didn't know that. It made me a tiny bit braver. About death.

That, I guess, was her last gift to me. Lopsided gift-giving if ever there was.

. . . .

I am saddest when I go to Agata & Valentina, a market in my neighborhood with the most delicious food, and I wander the aisles around sundown thinking about what I want for dinner. Nora loved to think about what she wanted for dinner. She should be here, buying some fresh mozzarella (salted), eyeing a sirloin, considering whether she wants crab cakes.

No, she wouldn't be here. I mean, she would probably send someone out for something she fancied. It's so hard not to know, only to be guessing. Right now I like to think she's at her desk, waiting for my call or about to call me.

BLAME IT ON
THE MOVIES

My twenties were one big walkabout.

There is, on television, a series called *Girls* about young women floundering in their twenties. It is written, directed, and acted by Lena Dunham, who is not on a walkabout. Nevertheless, she captures the very special misery of being in your twenties. Of being clueless, desperate, lost. Looking for love, settling for crazy. Grabbing at solutions because they are solutions, just not to your problem. Being in your twenties has changed a lot since I was in my twenties, but it is still a time when everything awful that happens is awful in a romantic way, even if you don't admit it (and you can't admit it because then you would be less important in the tragedy you're starring in, your own life) . . . because in your twenties you know, even if you don't admit this either, even if this is buried deep in your subconscious, that you can waste an entire decade and still have a life.

College did not prepare me for anything. At Barnard I majored in European history because my roommate, brilliant at history, always accurately guessed the exam essay questions. That is really the only reason. It was the easy way out. As I write this, I am struck by how shallow I was. A truly empty-headed thing. I was quick with a comeback, but a comeback is most emphatically not knowledge. Also when I was at Barnard, a European history major, unlike a political science or English major, was not required to take comprehensives, a general examination in your major at the end of your senior year. I knew I would flunk comprehensives. I retained nothing.

Recently I found a paper I wrote in college. "The Causes of the Franco-Prussian War." I got a B on it. I wondered if I pulled an all-nighter writing it. If I took NoDoz. If Susan, my roommate, told me the causes and I parroted her. Today all I know about this war is who fought it, and *that* is only because of the war's name. I wasn't interested in European history. It didn't cross my mind—this is so basic, it's embarrassing—that I was supposed to major in something I was interested in.

This is probably my mother's fault. Isn't everything your mother's fault in some way? At this point in life I forgive her everything and besides am deeply grateful to her, but she picked all my high school classes: two years of Latin, three of French, four of English and history, journalism as an elective. No science except what was absolutely required. Or art. She was raising writers. She had stern notions of what constituted an education for her daughters.

However, no one ever asked me—no parent, no teacher, no high school or college counselor—"What are you interested in studying?" I didn't connect interest with school. Or passion with school. In high school, the only class I liked was journalism. Not because I was writing. Because, for some reason, at Beverly Hills High School—a privileged place if ever there was, with its very own oil well polluting the environment and a basketball court whose floor parted in the center (if someone pushed a button or pulled a crank or lever) and retracted under bleachers to reveal a swimming pool—at this very fancy public school there was a linotype machine.

We're talking pre-computer age here. Whenever you read a book, a newspaper, a magazine, it was because the words were set with actual lead type. The linotype man would type my stories. The machine would convert my words to metal type, slugs of which, as I recall, came sliding down a chute. Lead type is heavy. If you carried a lot of type in your shoulder bag—not that you would—it would break your shoulder. How wonderful that it was heavy, that I could hold words in my hand and they had weight. I was the front-page editor, and Thursday nights I would go to the typesetting building next to the gym, collect my type, and arrange the page as I had designed it. After tightening the frame to hold the type in position, I would ink the whole shebang, place paper on top, and roll a heavy roller over it to get an impression. Then I would proofread my page, replace typos with new type, and take a final proof. It was the most fun in the world. It was craft satisfaction. Craft satisfaction comes from actually making something with your hands. In terms of education, it is practically obsolete.

In college the only thing that interested me was dating. Being in love. In the library I had a reward system: ten minutes of studying, ten of daydreaming. Mostly about whatever boy I was obsessed with, reliving the last weekend, planning the next. I have to say college completely cooperated here. Classes provided no competition for my yearnings. I took a course in plays, a foray out of history. We had to read a play a night. Strindberg, Ibsen, O'Casey, O'Neill, Wilder, went whizzing by. It's hard to read a play. Seriously hard to understand what is happening, what the playwright intends. Reading one a night was ludicrous. I still have trouble reading them, still have trouble now and then figuring out what the hell is going on. The final exam was a slew of multiple-choice questions. There was one about pork chops, which went something like this: "In which of these plays did pork chops figure?" All I knew about pork chops was, at my house, they came breaded with applesauce on the side. I had no idea what play featured pork chops. I still don't, but I remember the question. It was ridiculous. I retained ridiculous.

Modern Poetry was similar. Wednesday Wallace Stevens, Friday Ezra Pound. A person could spend a lifetime trying to understand Stevens, and Pound is mind-bendingly obtuse. In Medieval History, there was so much required reading, all in books the professor had written, that no one could accomplish it, especially someone like me who had required daydreaming. I did love Art History. I have never met anyone who didn't. I still remember the rush I got from correctly identifying a geometric shape at the bottom right corner of a Picasso as a cornucopia.

I hope kids are smarter about college now and colleges are smarter about educating them. I am longing to believe it (especially given how much college costs). When I was there, the sheer volume of homework made learning or getting excited about learning a steep uphill climb. My husband insists, even though I don't admit it, that I *was* learning—to think better, research, organize information, meet the demands of a deadline. At Connecticut College, where I spent two years before Barnard in small classes, that might have been true. But still I was wasting my parents' money. Wasting it big-time. It was, in retrospect, the life of a spoiled girl.

Getting married was a big part of my fantasy life. There was a card game called Old Maid that we played as kids. Each card had a partner card except one. The loser would be stuck with a card depicting a funny-looking gray-haired woman with glasses and a hat. The hat was especially sad—sort of a pillbox with a fake flower in it. Old Maid the card game struck terror in me. I was a superstitious kid, and getting left with that card seemed prophetic. There was also a song that freaked me out: "What Are You Doing New Year's Eve?" Ella Fitzgerald sang it (quite inappropriately, in my opinion) on a record of Christmas songs. When the record (what we now call *vinyl*, and why do we, it's so pretentious) got to that song, I would pick up the needle, very carefully so as not to scratch the record, and skip it to the next song. I couldn't bear to listen to it if I didn't have a date. Not having a date on New Year's Eve was like being an old maid. It was being an old maid every year.

This absurd hysteria about New Year's Eve stayed with me for much longer than I'd like to admit. Whenever I read about how people in their twenties don't date anymore, they travel in hordes, it makes me happy. Maybe this group thing has taken the sting out of New Year's Eve.

So, on the one hand, my mother was drilling me daily from the time I could hold a spoon: "You will have a career like me. You will work. You will be a writer. You will leave Los Angeles. You will go to New York City. You will work. Career, career, career." On the other hand—driving me as powerfully with no help from her—was simply wanting love.

I blame this on the movies. I blame it on one movie in particular: *Seven Brides for Seven Brothers*.

There were lots of messages keeping women domestic then, every message actually—lack of opportunity, advertising, the women's magazines like *McCall's*, *Ladies' Home Journal*, *Redbook*, *Seventeen*, which glorified the stay-at-home wife and which I devoured each month when they arrived at our house. But really the thing counteracting my mother's teaching, trumping it, was a singing and dancing 1950s romantic comedy starring pert blond Jane Powell.

In *Seven Brides for Seven Brothers*, Jane Powell is the cook at a roadhouse in a Wild West town when Howard Keel, big and handsome, rides in, shaves while he sings, samples her stew, and proposes. This is my favorite line: When he asks for catsup, she replies, "My stew can stand on its own feet." She agrees to marry him—it's love at first sight for her—and he takes her to his ranch in the backwoods, where she discovers he has six uncivilized (but sweet) brothers. It turns out she was looking for love, but he was looking for a servant. Boy, did I want to be that servant. Lucky Jane. She gets to rise at dawn, make flapjacks, eggs, bacon, biscuits, and coffee for eight (including her), wash their filthy clothes, and teach them to dance. Once cleaned up, they are gorgeous, and then— excuse me for telling the plot of this movie I love as much as I love my dog—she takes them to a barn raising, where they meet other town girls and fall in love. Those girls, however, are promised to less attractive town boys who wear stiff suits with dorky stitching on the lapels, while the brothers wear britches with wide leather belts and cool blousy shirts. The barn-raising musical number, choreographed by Michael Kidd, a dance-off between the townies and the brothers, is the greatest dance sequence in a movie ever. In my opinion.

The brothers return to the backwoods heartsick, so heartsick they can barely lift a pitchfork of straw. At Howard Keel's urging—stirring them to action as only a song can—they return one night and kidnap the women. A cute kidnapping, if you consider putting a bag over the head of someone you love cute. My favorite kidnap-cute from the film is not the bag-over-the-head, but this: When one young woman sets a hot pie on the windowsill to cool, she is whisked right out the window. I don't want to tell you the end of this movie in case you haven't seen it, although given the title, you can probably guess.

The movie came out when I was ten, and by the time I was twenty, I had seen it sixteen times. The last viewing was in Madrid. There were no subtitles, but it didn't matter because I knew it by heart.

It is the only movie of which I have counted my viewings. All sixteen were in one movie theater or another. I can't emphasize how important this is. Watching a movie in a theater is to enter a dream state. In *The Purple Rose of Cairo*, Woody Allen perfectly captures the transporting power of film. When Mia Farrow goes to the movies and is captivated by the glamorous world so different from the dismal small life she is living, her yearning is so great that the hero on-screen is pulled right out of his cinematic reality into her prosaic one.

I was young and vulnerable and innocent when I first saw *Seven Brides.* I took my heart into that theater and lost it.

Loving a movie is not about logic. If a movie "gets" me, I forgive it anything. If it doesn't, I sit there cold, critical, poking holes. I'm amazed that many sane people claim that violent movies don't make people more violent. This seems the delusional, self-serving justification of people who make violent movies. If violence excites you, a violent movie will nurture that. It must. Movies invite you to dream, change your dreams, become your dreams. Recently I was reading in the *New York Times* about Aton Edwards, a leader of the Prepper movement. Preppers are people who spend a lot of time preparing to survive a catastrophe, natural or terrorist, that results in an all-systems failure (banks, phones, food, transportation, breathing, whatever). Mr. Edwards said he went to see the movie *Deliverance* when he was ten years old . . . went in, according to the article, a fairly regular kid and emerged a Prepper.

"Ten" did pop out at me. I was ten when *Seven Brides* overwhelmed, seduced, and altered my life. He was ten when he saw *Deliverance*. I asked a developmental psychologist about ten. A big year, it turns out, when children first begin to think for themselves, entertaining ideas different from what their parents tell them. Budding sexuality, too. First feelings. *Deliverance* has a male rape in it—no wonder Edwards emerged a Prepper. I'm surprised more men didn't, but then it had an R rating. Ten-year-old Aton Edwards never should have been in that theater.

I do wonder if you spend your life preparing for disaster if you are disappointed if a disaster doesn't happen. If you are hoping for a disaster so you haven't wasted your time or can prove you're right or can finally have the adventure you crave or get to watch everyone else go down while you inflate your raft, load it up with gas masks and cans of tuna fish, and sail off Manhattan island (row, actually—row across the Hudson to New Jersey, are they kidding?).

The impact of *Seven Brides* was undoubtedly greater because I saw it in a theater as opposed to on a DVD, as opposed to lying on a bed, where I can say to whomever I'm watching with, "Would you please pause it? I want to get an apple."

As for romantic films being denigrated as chick flicks, consider this. My adolescent yearnings aside, when you're looking for love, aspiring to love, hoping for love, dreaming of love, movies are where it seems possible. When you're past the "falling" phase and in the calmer yet more complicated "being in love" (assuming you're committed to it), the only place you ever fall in love again is at the movies.

That is no small thing.

I blame my entire twenties walkabout on *Seven Brides.* On hoping some man was going to whisk me out a window and in the spring we would be singing with little baby lambs on our laps. (That happens, too, in *Seven Brides.* Oh God, I really do hope I haven't ruined the movie for you. I haven't even mentioned the fantastic sequence when the lonely brothers in the dead of winter sing "I'm a lonesome polecat." There, I've mentioned it. Although there is no ruining this movie. Trust a woman who has now seen it thirty times or more. I did eventually stop counting.)

When Howard Keel didn't show up, I pretended he did. I married the first man who asked me and began living someone else's life. Not Jane Powell's, but sort of. Marrying this man for misguided reasons wasn't the nicest thing to do to him, but, like Howard Keel, he had ulterior motives. Not wanting to be alone, I think. Besides, as you will soon see, while I wasted six years of his life, he wanted to wreck mine completely.

He was a professor at Brown University. Given how little I liked college, this was even weirder—I was a faculty wife living in a pretty but precious neighborhood around the university in Providence, Rhode Island.

While I had had no passion for Barnard, I had fallen head over heels for New York City. If New York is for you, nothing else will do. The beauty, the excitement, the friction. The thrill of mastery—not simply navigating the subway system, for instance, but knowing exactly where to get on a train so that, when you reach your destination and get off, you are exactly opposite the exit. I can't tell you how good that always makes me feel, that I know something that no one else knows except another New Yorker. Mostly, however, loving New York is personal: the validation of identity. New Yorkers are born all over the country and then they come to the city and it strikes them, "Oh, this is who I am."

At that time, I didn't have a clue who I was except that I was a New Yorker.

So there was this problem in my first marriage along with many others. I was actually in love with a city, not a person. No movie prepared me for city love. If one had,

I suspect it still would have been no match for *Seven Brides*.

My life in Providence was essentially false. I was pretending to be a helpmate (pretending that helpmate was a valid destiny, which for others it may be, but for me it wasn't). I was terrible at cleaning house. There is a saying: "If something is worth doing, it's worth doing well." It's not true. Housecleaning is only worth doing to the point that the place is clean enough that no one notices it's not.

I got a job as a Girl Friday.

A Girl Friday was a secretary with a BA. The term, which died sometime during the 1970s thanks to the Women's Liberation movement, is worth discussing because it's so insulting. In the classic, perhaps racist classic, *Robinson Crusoe* by Daniel Defoe (published in 1719), Friday was Robinson Crusoe's servant. Crusoe, shipwrecked and alone on an island, rescues a "savage" from death when a few cannibals canoe over to picnic on him. Crusoe names him Friday (after the day he saves him), thereby anticipating the creative baby-naming of the late twentieth and twenty-first centuries. Crusoe's name, he tells Friday, is Master. After that is settled and Friday has cleaned up the bones and flesh the other cannibals have left behind, Master teaches him other words like *yes* and *no*. Thus the origin of Girl Friday, a title intended to make a college-educated woman feel better about her menial job—better, that is, than another woman, a secretary.

I had this job at the Research and Design Institute.

In retrospect, I'm not sure what this company actually did. The guys who ran it claimed to design interior spaces, but they were not architects or designers. They were, they believed, better than that. More enlightened. It was a drink-the-Kool-Aid kind of place, and as for their designs, what I remember most was a lot of library shelving. The important thing was that my boss was mean. He lived to make underlings feel like shit. Picking on them, criticizing their work, causing them to anguish about whether they were about to be fired. Usually they were. This man was never mean to me, but here's what I learned and I pass on: A mean boss is eventually mean to everyone. One day he started ragging on me, something to do with the job he claimed I wasn't doing. It went on for a few weeks, and after one unpleasant attack, I picked up my purse and, as I passed him and some library shelving on the way to the exit, I said, "I quit." And he said, "You're flat-chested."

This is one of my favorite things that has ever happened to me. Because I love, love, love to tell it.

Only it is also one of those things . . . well, as I said, I was quick with a comeback, but in this case, to my life-long regret, I said nothing.

In any event, as a result, I was, at approximately twenty-seven years of age, unemployed and flat-chested.

What was I to do?

I went into the crochet business. This may not seem the obvious next move, although in *Seven Brides for Seven Brothers* Jane Powell knits. Knitting is harder than crocheting. My friend Lorrie taught me. We formed a business crocheting purses and belts for New York department stores. We landed a big order from Bendel. I had a week to crochet fifty purses. I was crocheting in my sleep. Two months after beginning, we flamed out.

Shortly thereafter, however, I was at a cocktail party in my beloved New York City, which I tried to escape to as much as possible, and met an editor from Simon & Schuster. I said to him, "I know you'd never be interested in this, but would you like a book about crocheting?"

He said, "Yes."

To my astonishment.

He must have been impressed by how confidently I presented myself.

That is how I got a contract for my first book, *The Adventurous Crocheter.* My friend illustrated it and I wrote it. Well, "writing" is an overstatement for what I was doing, mostly instructions for how to make purses, belts, and sweaters. At this point it was dawning on me that I have one life—dawning not in an abstract way, which was the way I'd always understood it, but like a brick falling on my head. There wasn't an actual brick— by that I mean there was no eureka. It didn't happen on a birthday. I didn't see someone on the street that I didn't want to be in ten years or someone that I did. Partly you can fake being someone you're not for only so long, al- though it's easier if you don't know who you are to begin with. Partly thirty coming at me made this impossible to ignore: I had one life and I was fucking it up. (A caveat: I didn't think I was fucking it up, even though that's what I was doing, because we didn't use the word *fuck* in the seventies the way we do now every thirty seconds.) I had one life and I was screwing it up. That realization didn't make me brave, but brave enough to take some baby steps.

While I was writing a second book, *Gladrags,* again mainly instructions, this time about remaking clothes— still mining the pioneer woman fantasy—a bigger dream was surfacing that had to do with the real me. I said to my husband—my first husband, that's important here—I said to him, "You know, I really think I'd like to try to be a writer."

And he said, "I don't want you to be a writer."

And I said, "Why?"

And he said, "I don't want you to be famous. Suppose you become famous?"

And I said, "I promise I won't be famous."

I wonder to this day, because I am a faithful sort of person, if I did keep that promise. But obviously if your husband wants to crush your tender dream with his big fat foot (even if you're Jane Powell), you have to leave him. So I did.

We sold our house and made a modest profit. If I lived cheaply, I figured that I had two years to become a writer.

(It is only now that I realize that this ambition/drive/ bravery to become a writer surfaced *after* I had written one book and was in the middle of a second. I suppose I didn't consider my craft writing "writing." I still don't. But I am very attached to *The Adventurous Crocheter.* I know some of it by heart. "There is no wrong way to cro-chet. There are easier ways and harder ways, but any way is right as long as the work looks and acts like crochet-ing." The reason I remember these lines is that, while my husband was telling me he didn't want me to become a writer, I recited them to myself silently like a mantra blocking his voice.)

So, my plan—two years. In two years I had to become a self-supporting writer. Otherwise I'd have to find something else to do. It's important to have a plan when one is creating that much upheaval. Nevertheless, I was terrified. My marriage hadn't been nurturing or even supportive, but it was secure. Now I was flying blind. Fortunately I was moving back to New York City and the loving care of my girlfriends.

My friend Lorrie met me at Penn Station. We went up to my friend Susan's, where Lorrie made me dinner— she always made amazing food, had actually baked my three-tiered wedding cake, and now was making me a divorce salad, as I recall with shrimp. Susan, who had been my college roommate, was happy to have me camp forever on her pullout couch, but she was of such a generous nature that soon there were three more living there (I was the only one getting divorced or it would have been a television series). The building took offense and we had to move out.

I then moved up to my friend Jean's large apartment on the Upper West Side. Jean had replaced her couches with hammocks that swung from the living room ceiling.

That wasn't a problem, although it was strange visually and meant if you shared a hammock with someone, you were practically having sex. Her ex-husband had built the dining room chairs, which didn't have legs but triangle bases. If you shifted even slightly in your seat while eating, you crashed to the floor. That wasn't the problem, either. The problem was she didn't believe in killing roaches with poison. She sprinkled around herbal things. For roaches, this stuff was testosterone.

While I wasn't going back to Rhode Island, I was having trouble moving forward. The feeling I remember most from that time was displacement: Wherever I was, was wrong. I would be visiting someone and think, *I have to leave. I have to get out of here.* I'd get somewhere else and feel the same. Something was missing—home. Living with friends prolonged that feeling. Kept me in limbo, which was exactly right. Not wanting to go backward, unable to move forward. At the same time I was exhilarated. At least I was no longer spending all day every day deciding whether or not to leave. There was so much more room in my brain.

I spent most of the summer like this—in a dazed, mostly happy paralysis—and then in the fall found a place of my own and settled in.

Also.

There is something fantastic about getting divorced. Everyone should do it to experience the extraordinary sense of freedom after being in marriage jail. I take that back. (Sometimes I write something and all I can think about is how many people on Twitter are going to dump on me for it.) Divorce is a catastrophe under many circumstances, like if you have children. Or if you don't want it. Or have no money. Just to name a very few. But if you do want it and you're (still) young: adventure, passion awaits. One simply radiates heat, and that, along with a reckless, uninhibited joy, lasts at least three months, sometimes six.

When I was down to my last $300, which would have been $500 except I fell in love with an orange coat, I was sitting at home one night eating chocolate pudding. It was the kind of pudding you cook—the kind that has skin on the top. I was eating it the way I always had: making a little hole in the skin, scooping the soft pudding out from underneath, saving the skin for last. I was eating like a child. I wrote about it—five hundred words about how children eat food. It was in the form of instructions. I was good at instructions. I sold "How to Eat Like a Child" to the *New York Times*. It appeared on the back page of the

Sunday magazine, and magically, unimaginably, on Monday I was offered a book contract. Officially, I was a writer. I was launched.

Sort of. I don't want to gloss over this. There was the little problem of having no work habits. No one can become anything without discipline, that's the truth. I had a shrink at the time, which will come as no surprise and was the other reason I was down to my last $300. He said, and I pass this on to any aspiring writers, that I had to sit down at my desk every day from ten to twelve. I didn't have to write, but I couldn't get up, feed my plants, make tea, phone a friend. I had to keep my butt in the seat. Then I had to do the same thing from two to four. It works. You write. And it takes the question "Will I write?" out of your day. It turns writing into habit.

And then, just before my book (*How to Eat Like a Child and Other Lessons in Not Being a Grown-up*) was published, my life changed, thanks to the movies.

In the late 1970s, which it was now, some movies were more realistic when it came to women's lives and were not something a girl could blame an entire lost decade on. *An Unmarried Woman*, starring Jill Clayburgh, was about a thirty-something New York City woman and her life after divorce. In other words, it was about me. I didn't identify with Jill Clayburgh's character, however, and not because she jogged in the movie and I could never identify with anyone who jogs. I was over movie heroines. I was figuring out who I was. No more screen fantasies. I had learned my lesson. I was done.

My girlfriend Amy and her friend—a guy I had never met—went to see this movie, but it was sold out. The theater was in my neighborhood. Amy said—this is the way Jerry tells it—she said to him, "I have this friend you will absolutely love."

Which turned out to be true.

They stopped by, and I peered down over the banister as they came up the stairs to my very adorable third floor walk-up—the sort of place a romantic comedy heroine would live, above a Burger Heaven and a beauty salon. I took one look at Jerry and lost my heart.

There was no Wild West, no stew, and no brothers, but it was just like Jane. Instantaneous.

NAME-JACKED

A couple of years ago I was name-jacked.

I hadn't looked at my website in a while, having nothing new to add, but I thought, *I have a novel coming out, I should bring it up to date.* So I Googled "deliaephron.com" and it wasn't there. Instead there was a message: *This domain is for sale.*

I called the person in charge of my website, who happens to be a family member, and he had neglected to renew the website for reasons having to do with changing his e-mail and credit card. "Don't worry," he said. "We have a day left to get it back." But we did not. When we tried to buy it, someone else already had.

Someone else owned my name. Someone could use my name to say or show pretty much anything they wanted. I felt . . . I won't say *raped*, I'm not crazy, but I did feel violated. That same week I had an appointment with my doctor. It turned out she had been name-jacked, too. "It's no big deal," she told me. "It's a scam. You just have to buy it back."

As soon as I got home I rushed over to Digital Society, my local Apple specialist, to consult Mike Rowe, the owner. "What could they want with my name? I'm not famous—I can't even get a reservation at ABC Kitchen. Could I end up a porn site?" Mike didn't answer, just kind of *hmm*ed, as in, *Don't go there yet.* He advised me to hire Go Daddy, an Internet company with a domain buying service that gets hijacked names back. You tell them how much you're willing to pay, they locate the person who name-jacked you and make the exchange— money for your domain (which is rightfully yours to begin with).

Which raised the question: How much was my name worth to me? Was it worth more than a flat-screen TV, more than a month's rent? Would I pay $5,000 for my name? $10,000? While I was trying to decide, Go Daddy appraised my name and advised me it was worth $68.

In the meantime, I went into a domain-buying

frenzy. I bought deliaephron.net, delia-ephron.com, deliaephron.name.

Of course, the anxiety wasn't just what the name-jacker would do with my name, but what I would do without it. In this world of self-promotion, where writers are expected to do at least as much marketing as their publishers, how could anyone who presumably liked one of my books find out more about me, like why I wrote it or that I have a dog named Honey? Or, conveniently, find out what else I had written and buy it with a click?

My mother made a huge fuss about her daughters' names. She bragged often, "My girls have names no one else has." Now I had a name someone else had. Someone from Japan. Because very soon, when I Googled "delia ephron.com," a site popped up in Japanese.

The Web can freak you out, and I freak easily. So I never clicked on the site, and asked a friend who spoke Japanese to translate. I thought I might get hooked in a bad way, like tracking on Facebook some guy who'd done you wrong. But I was raging. What a way to make a living—going around stealing people's names. What a cipher-ish thing to do. Really, think about it. I did, night and day.

After several weeks, Go Daddy informed me that they were not able to make contact with my current domain owner. They would continue for another month, but prospects were low.

Now the question became, did I want to sue?

I did. I was angry and I really wanted my name back. It represented my life—my hard work, my accomplishments, my point of view, my mother's originality. I guess I was proud of it. I certainly didn't want anyone exploiting it.

Jeffry Weicher, my new website designer who was not a family member, explained that I had to file a claim with WIPO, the World Intellectual Property Organization, located in Geneva. Through Jeffry Weicher, I found Patrick Bergin, a Milwaukee attorney who specialized in intellectual property law. Mr. Bergin determined that the owner had registered my domain with a German registrar to make it harder for us to identify him. So now I was suing a Japanese person (or company) registered in Germany in a Swiss court with a Milwaukee lawyer.

I told Mr. Bergin about all the domain names I owned. He said a .com was far preferable to a .net. He suggested, while we were waiting for this to play out, which could take months, I use deliaephronwriter.com, although many friends following this saga said it was too many letters to expect someone to type. Still, it was clearly me.

While I was suing, I had a new website built, but here's the thing: Just because you have a website doesn't mean anyone can find it. I Googled myself and still got only the Japanese site. My other site had been in operation six years; it was embedded in Google. To counteract this, Jeffry Weicher instructed, I had to contact anyone who had the old hijacked website listed—like Wikipedia, various publishers, IMDb—and give them the new website name.

Can't you just call up Google and explain, "Hey, when I put my name in, the right site doesn't come up, the false site does"? You can't. I was effectively deep-sixed. Google my name and my new site would only turn up on page two, three, four, or five, and who was going to go to that much trouble to find me except my husband, who already knew where I was?

The cost of suing, estimated to be slightly more than $3,500, went higher when we had to protest a request from WIPO to translate our brief into Japanese. The brief we filed—"a short plain statement," my lawyer called it—claimed that my name was well-enough known to be, in effect, a trademark. It delineated my credits. "I tried to hit the highlights," he said. My name, the brief concluded, was being used "in bad faith" for what is called a "parking site." A parking site means, Google me and you can click to buy products that have nothing to do with me.

Six months later, WIPO ruled in my favor, in part, according to the decision, because it was "a personal name that is both well-known and relatively rare." Thank you, Mom.

The transfer would take a few weeks. In the meantime, my site would be in transition. When I Googled "deliaephron.com," the link appeared to be slightly different, although still in Japanese. The great Google engine had acknowledged something, but what? I noticed an option to translate. I clicked on it. In a few seconds the translation appeared. The headline read, and I quote exactly, "Measures Under The Safest Mutual Link Link." The first line read, and I quote exactly, "Recently Google has become stricter measures link to the site have been under an spam."

It takes a while for Google to catch up, according to my website expert. It took two more weeks, actually. And not that Google cares—I mean, it's not as if I can call them up and tell them—but they should hire another Japanese translator.

THE BANKS
TAKETH

B anks are eating up all the real estate in my neighborhood. I live on a basically residential street, and
within three and a half short blocks of my house are eight
banks: two Chase, one Wells Fargo, one Citibank, one
HSBC, one Bank of America, one Sovereign, and one
Capital One. Go two more blocks and there are ten banks
(one more Chase and one more Citibank).

Why are the banks paying only 0.4 percent interest
on a savings account if they can afford to open offices on
every other block in Greenwich Village?

The other day I was catching up on balancing my
account and realized that, for the last six months, I had

earned about $4 in interest but had been charged $35 a
month for service.

I went to the bank at the corner (the southwest corner). "This is insane," I said.

The banker explained that I had a service charge because I didn't maintain a high enough balance.

"At this rate I will have no balance. Besides, what
about my CD? I have a CD here."

"Oh," he said, looking it up on the computer. "Someone forgot to bundle that in."

"Reverse the charges," I said, and he said that they
could reverse three months but not six. To get all six reversed I had to go to my originating branch.

"This is my originating branch," I said.

"No, it isn't."

"Yes, it is. I opened my account here. I live down the
block."

"Sorry. You have to go to your originating branch at
79th and Broadway."

Now, I had shut down an account on the Upper West
Side about a decade ago and, after a six-year break,
opened a new one when I moved downtown. But even if
there was some justification for their confusion, that
wasn't the point.

"There are three branches within walking distance,

but I have to take two subways to reverse my charges? That is insane."

Insane is what I said, but actually it was fishy.

"Call them and tell them to reverse the charges," I said.

"You have to do it in person."

At that point I threatened to withdraw my meager savings from the bank. The bank manager appeared, reversed the charges for all six months, and gave me his card. "Let us invest for you," he said.

"Why would I let you do that?"

"Because you're not earning anything on your money."

Not the next day, but practically, my husband went to his bank's ATM at the corner (the southeast corner) to withdraw money from his business account, and his card, which he hadn't used for a while, was rejected. He went into his bank.

"You're not on the account," he was told.

"Who is?"

"No one," said the banker.

"But how is that possible?" said my husband. "I've had this account for thirty years. You won't even open an account without a signatory."

"The computer must have lost your name."

"How?"

After pressing a few buttons on her keyboard and scrolling around, she gave up and speculated that this must have happened when Wells Fargo ate Wachovia. "You have to prove that the company is yours," she said. "Until then, you can deposit money but you can't withdraw."

Proving it involved a call to his lawyer, who had to locate my husband's articles of incorporation in storage, and a bill for $145, which—after my husband threatened to withdraw his money—the bank agreed to pay.

"This is insane," he told them, but later pointed out that actually, from the bank's point of view, it was brilliant: a bank where you can only deposit.

Which perhaps explains what all these new branches are for. Since no one needs to go into a bank to withdraw money, simply to the ATM, the banks must be in the business of taking our money but not in the business of giving it back.

I don't have credit card debt because Suze Orman advises against it, but I was having lunch with a friend the other day who was a wreck because her bank charges 18 percent interest. There was no way she could ever pay down her credit card debt. So I was thinking that all of us earning 0.4 percent could instead loan money to our friends at 0.5 percent. It was a bit odd thinking of myself as a benevolent loan shark, but, hey, my friend would get out of debt, I would earn $5 a month instead of $4, and the banks would make so much less money that they would have to close half their branches and give us our city back.

I mentioned the idea to my accountant, who told me it was insane. "You can't trust your friends," he said.

HIT & RUN

One Friday evening, my dog, Honey, was taking a walk with her dog walker, Lauren, when she was clipped by a car.

Honey bolted, yanking the leash out of Lauren's hand—apparently dogs get a huge surge of adrenaline after being hit by cars. If they survive, they take off, running even on broken legs, ruptured insides, whatever.

Several people chased after her and after the car, which slowed for a moment and then sped off down Seventh Avenue. A total stranger named David Zeh photographed the license plate. Then he flagged a cab and got Honey, Lauren, and Ayana (another dog walker, who managed to capture Honey) to the Fifth Avenue

Veterinary Specialists—a twenty-four-hour emergency hospital with an amazing trauma team. The second night, she was able to lift her head. Two weeks later, she was home on bed rest recovering with several cracked ribs and leg wounds.

Since this happened, two people have told me that their feet were run over by taxicabs and a third that a cab took off while she was getting out of it, tossing her onto the sidewalk. But this isn't about taxis. I mention this only because I am astonished that it was not a cab that hit Honey, given the maniac drivers and the endless telephone talking that they do even though it's illegal. This is about how nice everyone in this city is: the New Yorkers who chased the car and my dog, the Good Samaritan, Mr. Zeh, the couple in the waiting room whose pit bull had broken out in hives and needed a shot of Benadryl, the animal hospital staffed with surgeons who didn't become surgeons because they hate to speak to people. And my apartment building, too.

Word traveled quickly, and all the dog lovers in the building asked about Honey. In most cases I know their dogs' names, not theirs—Moki, Biscuit, Jack, Maisie—and they know Honey's name, not mine, because the thing about apartment living is that neighbors are friendly but not friends. An apartment building provides a comfort zone, a bit of padding between you and the city, a reminder when it counts that the city is not about the driver who hit Honey and kept going, but about folks who care about what happens to your dog.

An apartment building is a little like Facebook. It seemed a bit crazy to me that I posted news of Honey's accident on my Wall, but her photo is on my Wall. Her photo is where my photo is supposed to be. Many Facebook friends (most of whom I have never met) posted good wishes, and I was grateful. No one wrote, *I hope your dog dies, dude.* But then, I'm not a teenager. I suppose Facebook is a kind of Internet apartment building, providing a bit of padding between you and whatever might pop up about you on the Web.

I called 311 to find out if hitting a dog was a crime and was referred to the 6th Precinct. According to a dog owner working there, the police would not arrest the driver. Dogs are property (hence the term "dog owner"). The offense was, I assume, civil, not criminal. And therefore that driver can go on hitting dogs and getting away with it.

AM I JEWISH
ENOUGH?

This question occurred to me when my publisher
asked if I wanted to be on the JBC circuit.

I had never heard of it.

My publisher explained. The Jewish Book Council
sponsors book festivals in cities around the country. The
festivals—usually from the middle of October to the middle of November—feature Jewish authors or authors who
have written on Jewish subjects.

I have never thought of myself as a Jewish author. I
am an author who happens to be Jewish. I have never
written a Jewish heroine, for instance. Although I have
written a few who were half Jewish, none of them were
practicing Jews.

My publisher explained how the JBC circuit works. You have to try out. "Pitch yourself." Then, if they like you—"they" being the people who run these festivals— they will invite you to give a talk. If the audience enjoys your talk, they presumably will buy your book, which will be for sale afterward.

To sum up: You pitch yourself to win the honor of pitching yourself. It seemed demeaning.

However, I love my book. All authors do. My book is my baby, and I am a helicopter parent, certain that without constant supervision/support/interfering/flag-waving/cheerleading/tweeting/Facebooking, my book doesn't stand a chance in this cruel, cold, increasingly short-attention-span world. I also know this because my publisher says so.

Pitching to the JBC is the least I can do for my baby.

My publisher kindly filled out the application form for me and paid the $365 entry fee. The JBC charges for the right to pitch to win the honor of pitching.

I then started receiving JBC e-mails and phone calls with instructions. I would have exactly two minutes to sell myself. If I went over, they would cut me off. Someone would hold up a sign at one minute and again at thirty seconds. No speaking from notes. One famous writer read his pitch off an iPad, the JBC representative told me, and no one wanted him.

A few weeks later, by appointment, a woman called to screen my pitch. I passed—no surprise, having been trained at the Ephron dinner table, where every time I said something funny, my dad shouted, "That's a great line, write it down."

Over the course of two days in June, the woman explained, four groups of sixty (that's 240 Jewish writers) would gather at the Hebrew Union College to compete. A Jewish Hunger Games, I suppose. The last time I was part of a group pitch, I was a junior at Beverly Hills High School, hoping to become an exchange student in Brazil. Thank God I didn't get it. I was sure that I would have to sweep a floor, and my mother told me never to learn to housekeep because someone might ask me to do it.

Which brings me to my mother.

My mother was violently opposed to organized religion. "Religion is the cause of all wars," she declared regularly. It wasn't true, but it sounded true. She was prescient, however, because these days it is true.

Beverly Hills, where I grew up (1950s and 1960s), was primarily Jewish. On Jewish holidays I was the only kid in class except for my friend Stephanie, who was Catholic.

Delia Ephron

Until eighth grade, when boys had their Bar Mitzvahs, I never entered a temple. Many Bar Mitzvahs were awesomely long. I learned to skip the first hour and a half and sneak in for the last forty minutes or so. When I grew up and moved to New York City, I knew that Yom Kippur (the holy day of atonement) was the best day to get a hard-to-score dinner reservation. More than once I have said, "It's Yom Kippur, we can get in anywhere."

My family celebrated Christmas. We always bought a tree that was too tall and had to saw off the top. We decorated it on Christmas Eve. My dad always had a swearing fit because the lights were tangled, and my mother was always telling us not to throw tinsel but to hang it. I read my large illustrated copy of *The Night Before Christmas*, the poem by Clement Moore, to tatters and can still recite it by heart. Which isn't that big a deal. I can also recite "Old Ironsides," "Casey at the Bat," and the Gettysburg Address, all of which I had to memorize at El Rodeo, my elementary school.

My family sang carols, too. "O Holy Night" was one of my favorites.

The subject of Christ and the manger, however, never came up, except in song.

On the other hand, in our family, *Volkswagen* was a four-letter word. I was counseled never ever to buy

86

German. I had nightmares about the Holocaust, especially this thing I heard about there being a line of prisoners and some were sent to the gas chambers and some were not. You live, you die. I had a mouth full of gold fillings and was sure, if I were ever in a concentration camp, all my gold would be extracted without Novocain. I may have been raised in a family of agnostics, but I knew that if the Jews got rounded up again, I would get rounded up, too.

We were secular. Not only did we not practice the Jewish religion, to my memory, we never discussed heaven, hell, faith, the bible, God. The Old Testament did come up once, as I recall. My parents, who were a screenwriting team, told us that in the movie *The Ten Commandments*, the Red Sea was actually Jell-O. The filmmakers had made the sea part, they said, by pouring the Jell-O in and then running the film backward.

Twice in my life I converted to Christianity. Once by accident. Once because my husband told me, "Just do it, it's no big deal."

The first time I was seventeen. The Reverend Billy Graham was having a rally in the Los Angeles Coliseum, and my friend Stephanie and I went out of curiosity. We sat high in the packed bleachers and listened to him preach. We expected to see something out of

Elmer Gantry, a movie about a charismatic revivalist (con man), featuring stomping, singing, religious faints. We were disappointed. Graham wasn't charismatic or rabble-rousing. He was ordinary, boring even, matter-of-fact. Flat.

Many of those around us, who felt otherwise, said they had come to hear him many times, and when Graham asked us all to "put a brick in his church"—a phrase that has stuck with me—a large plastic container traveled down the rows, and everyone except us threw in a dollar (which was worth a lot more then).

Stephanie and I hadn't brought binoculars, and Graham was a mere speck. When he said, "If you believe, come down here," and people began to pour down the aisles and gather in the bowl of the Coliseum, we decided to join them to get a closer look.

While we were milling around on the grass, still without much of a view because of the crowd, Graham said, "Now that you have given yourself to Christ . . ."

That came as a shock.

I had no idea that simply by leaving my seat I had given myself to Christ.

He continued, ". . . one of our advisors will help you get started on your new life."

A man grabbed my arm. Another grabbed Stephanie's.

I realized that many of the folks who'd poured down the aisles were working for the reverend.

"When did you begin to believe?" the man asked me. He sort of boomed the question. Like he was God from above, only he was standing right next to me.

"When did you?" I asked.

I wasn't being brash. This was more of a panicked defensive move, because I thought he expected some booming back from me. I remember the trapped feeling so clearly, because it was one of those teenage moments when you pull off a goof (which I liked to do now and then) and get way more than you bargained for.

My "advisor" told me about his realization that Christ died on the cross for him, and then he asked my name, address, and phone number. I gave fake ones—the name Annette Sorenson comes to mind (I thought it was Swedish). He handed me a fill-in-the-blank book to get me started on my new life.

He helped me with the first question, which he read aloud. "Who have sinned?" He filled in, "All have sinned."

I said that my mother was expecting me home, pulled Stephanie away from her advisor, and we left.

My parents loved the story. I told it that night at dinner and got big laughs.

Then in 2010, my husband and I were asked to be godparents. I was already a godparent twice over, one child was half Jewish, the other was Anglican. In those instances, our friends, the parents of our godchildren, never mentioned religion. I assumed that being a godparent meant taking an extra special interest in the child of someone you love, although I also remembered that Jenny Sullivan's godfather (her parents were friends of my parents) gave her a car for her sweet sixteen. I had no plans to give my godchildren cars.

In this case, however, we were invited to the baptism ceremony in an Episcopal church in Connecticut.

When we arrived, we all gathered near the altar: the parents, our six-month-old godson, Teddy, in an adorable white baptism outfit, my husband and I, and the minister, who was a woman.

The minister prepared us for the ceremony. It would take place during the service in front of the congregation. Among the many questions she was going to ask—which included "Will you renounce Satan?" and "Will you be responsible for seeing that your godson is raised in the Christian faith?"—was this one: "Do you turn to Jesus Christ and accept him as your Savior?"

I must have made a strange face, because I saw Teddy's mom, whom I love, blanch, and I thought, *She is worried that I am about to wreck the baptism*, which I was. I was thinking, *No way*.

"And you answer, 'I will,'" said the minister.

"I can't do this," I whispered to my husband, who is Jewish but does not take religion seriously in any way. To him it's all mumbo jumbo.

"Just do it, what does it matter, it's no big deal, it's only words," said Jerry.

"Only words? Words are my life."

But I did. Sort of. Well, I intended to, but during the ceremony Teddy had a screaming fit. He turned red, he squirmed and kicked, he had to be carried out of the church to calm down. He had never thrown a tantrum like that in his life. When it came to the big question, "Will you turn to Jesus?" no one heard me add a "not" very softly after I said, "I will." My husband answered, "I will," so I guess as a result he converted and now we have a mixed marriage.

. . . .

The first time I got married, I married a Gentile. More specifically, a WASP. The ceremony was in a judge's chambers. I was twenty-five. We had no discussions about faith or going to a church or temple or raising children in one religion or another. Still, in spite of the lack of interest in religion that we shared, to me his family was foreign. It was, for instance, at his parents' dinner table that I first heard the expression "gentlemen's grades." Which were Cs. A compliment for a C is not in a Jew's vocabulary.

I felt out of place at his parents' home, although in truth it wasn't all that different from ours, except his parents were not alcoholics. I'm sorry to say mine were by this time, having sadly blown on drink what seems to me an amazingly blessed life. Then, perhaps still, alcoholism was associated more with WASPs than Jews (one more way my parents assimilated)—WASPs who drank martinis. I'm generalizing, *ça va sans dire*, but you have only to watch *Seinfeld*—remember Susan's parents? (Actually you have only to watch *Seinfeld* to know everything. There is a *Seinfeld* episode for every single thing that happens in life, which is a remarkable achievement.)

My first husband's father served dinner from a silver platter, and when he did, he always said to me, "What can I do you for?" At every dinner I knew it was coming. "What can I do you for?" I began to dread it, an overreaction to the foolish place I found myself by marrying the first man who asked me as a way of avoiding . . .

absolutely everything, from becoming a writer to falling
in love. "What can I do you for?"—a joke that not only
wasn't funny but, worse, involved bad grammar. How did
this happen?

No question, I had an inbred arrogance about the culture I was raised in, about the worship of books, theater,
writing, and brains. My mother often said proudly, "We
have books in every room." Yes, floor-to-ceiling shelves
galore crammed with books. There were no artfully
placed *objets* on our shelves. Every ounce of space was for
the written word. My mother was a grammar fanatic, too.
I still remember this sentence she repeatedly used to
demonstrate a misplaced modifier. "I saw a man riding a
bicycle with a broken leg."

One Sunday morning when I was at my first husband's parents' house, which had few enough book-
shelves that I can't recall them, we had eaten breakfast,
were hanging out reading the newspaper, and his mother
kept asking, "Where's the gardening section? Who has
the gardening section?" I didn't answer. I was reading
the theater section. Even though I read the *New York
Times* every Sunday, I had no idea that, at that time, the
last few pages of the Arts and Leisure section, which
my family called the theater section, were devoted to

flowers, bulbs, and soil. Calling the theater section the gardening section? I knew from that alone I was in the wrong family.

At the JBC tryouts, there were no authors pitching books about intermarriage, but there were several about leaving orthodoxy. The woman who left, the gay who left, the transsexual who left.

And I must say, while sitting there in the auditorium alphabetized between, I believe, Eisenberg and Feldman, I felt the oppression of religion. Of any organization that gathers us together because we're one religion and not another. Because what I really think is that there is too much religion these days. Too much "I'm this and you're that." Fanatics are everywhere. I read a *New York Times* opinion piece by Frank Bruni about a cadet who left West Point in protest because he was pressured to participate in born-again religious services. Boy, that's who I want defending my free country, religious zealots. At orthodox Jewish temples, women must sit separately from men, upstairs or on the other side of the room, separated by a partition. That offends me.

While it is great to be part of a Jewish culture that reveres books enough to hold festivals, religion has nothing to do with why or how I choose friends, select books to read, or decide where to live or whom to vote for or love.

My mother, however, has everything to do with it.

. . . .

My grandmother, a Russian immigrant, was a dumpling of a woman with a doleful face and long gray hair that she twisted into a bun. She always entered our house by the back door. Perhaps she was intimidated by her assimilated daughter's glamorous Beverly Hills life. She didn't hear very well, which must have increased her isolation. I remember saying, "Hi, Grandma, how are you?" and her replying, "Bacon and eggs, as usual." She spent most of her time in the kitchen making chopped liver and the most delicious cinnamon cookies, although one of her best concoctions had a distinctly Gentile ring to it: spaghetti with a sauce of Campbell's tomato soup (made with milk, not water). I've always suspected that, for immigrant Jews, Campbell's symbolized America. More than religious freedom. More than Chinese food. Waiting to greet them after months of seasickness, tuberculosis, death in steerage, were the original five: the tomato, the vegetable, the chicken, the consommé, and the oxtail (although I can't believe my grandma was interested in the consommé or the oxtail). Lady Liberty, her arm raised, could have been carrying not a torch but a can of Campbell's.

In any event, I digress, because the memory I was summoning is this: When I was about twelve, my parents bought a painting, and when my grandmother and I were checking it out, newly hung in the den, she asked me if the painter was Jewish. I thought that was so funny. It was such an irrelevant question.

The oppression of organized religion is a theme in the novel I have written, the novel that I am at the JBC tryouts to talk about, although I leave that out of the two-minute pitch. For one thing, one of my heroines is a Southern Baptist who leaves her preacher husband. So not Jewish. Not-Jewish does not seem the way to go here.

In fact, after the pitch session, when we were all mingling, a representative from one of the Jewish book festivals asked if I had any Jewish characters in my novel, and I was forced to confess, no.

Forced to confess, I say, because what trumps everything for an author is wanting to sell books. I knew I had just sold one less.

A month or so after the group pitch, I was notified that I had received several invitations and I began that fall to travel to Jewish book festivals. As a result, I found myself not exactly deep in questions of Jewish identity, but peripherally circling them, sort of on the level of Woody Allen's character in the film *Hannah and Her Sisters*: Having a nervous breakdown and investigating Christianity, he discovers mayonnaise.

What does Judaism mean to me? Did I have a Jewish upbringing? How religious am I? These questions came from people I met as well as from magazine or newspaper reporters interviewing me for publicity in advance of my arrival.

I was stumped, because I am an author who happens to be Jewish and hadn't given it thought, but I understood that if a person attends a Jewish book festival, that person certainly had.

I consulted Jewish friends. "What does Judaism mean to you?" "Culture and pickles," said one who was writing a biography about a Catholic saint. Someone else said that her family called themselves "comedy Jews," which she added really meant that they were atheists. Another suggested that I sidestep the question by saying my family's religion was show business. This was true— my dad told endless Hollywood stories. He was in love with being a screenwriter and the world of moviemaking. I tried that answer, but got a follow-up. "Are you a food

Jew?" the reporter asked. I considered. Not really. While we ate nova and bagels every Sunday, I didn't taste a matzo ball until I was forty. "A book Jew," I offered.

While in Indianapolis, I was picked up at the airport by a lovely woman and delivered to a talk. When we missed the exit and practically ended up in Chicago, we started discussing how much we loved the telephone directory, that Texas-sized stack of pages that got dropped on your doorstep every year until Google rendered it useless. Whenever she traveled, she said, she always looked up her last name in the local white pages. She wanted to see how many Jews with her last name—very distant relatives, she assumed—lived there and where. She didn't phone them up. She was simply curious. She liked knowing they were there.

I have an affection for the phone book because, when my nephews were nine and ten and could barely see above the wheel, I took them to the huge veterans' cemetery in West Los Angeles, sat them on top of the Los Angeles white pages, and let them drive my Honda.

The official white or yellow pages is also the best way to kill a bug.

I am terrified of bugs, especially roaches and their larger relatives, water bugs. Once I woke up from a nap and there was a water bug on my arm. I levitated off the bed and crashed onto the floor. My head narrowly missed the wrought iron edge of a table, which seemed a miracle. That sort of miracle, surviving a water bug, is my kind of miracle—the kind I could entertain my parents with.

In any event, the most effective way to kill a bug without having to get near it is to drop or throw a white pages on it. In my thirties, when I was single, I got very good at this. My aim was unerring. (The only thing I do remotely as well is parallel park.) When the white pages stopped arriving, I switched to *The Gourmet Cookbook*, a huge two-volume tome my mother gave me.

The other way to kill a bug is to invite a Gentile over to do it. Which, when I was single, I also occasionally did.

As I began my talk at a festival in another Midwestern city, I immediately noticed a *farbissina*. This Yiddish word that my husband taught me means "bitter woman." She was sitting smack-dab in front of me in the front row, an intimidating presence, with her arms crossed over her chest, her breasts hiked up over them. If you included her elbows, she took up three seats.

She was muttering a lot, although I didn't quite hear her comments until I began speaking of my mother.

My mother believed in nonconformity. We, her

daughters, were expected to be nonconformists, too, which essentially meant we had to conform to everything she said. Still, it was fantastic because her rules called into question everything that was common wisdom at the time. Number one, you will have careers.

She was the only working mother we knew. The only one, and she was proud of it. "Your mother works, and you will, too." Remember how Hillary Clinton was excoriated for saying she was no cookie-baking, stand-by-your-man Tammy Wynette, and she rushed to backtrack? My mother was unapologetically no cookie-baking Tammy Wynette.

"Don't worship celebrities, they're no better than you are," she also told us. This was my favorite: "Just because you're related to someone is no reason to like them." Most mothers did not give their kids license to hate them. This rule captures my mother more than any—she was deeply unsentimental. And this is useful for writers—more than useful, necessary. It gave me permission to feel what I wanted, not to feel guilty, to accept and explore the truth in life or fiction. "Never buy on sale" was another.

When I said, "Never buy on sale," the *farbissina*, who had been keeping up a running commentary, said quite loudly, "Anti-Semitic."

I felt I had to address that heckle immediately. It

was provocative, rude, and it made me defensive. My
mother wasn't anti-Semitic, I said. She was proud to earn
money, to have become successful, and delighted to find
herself, through her own talent and hard work, living in
a large house in Beverly Hills, basking in the Southern
California sun. She was thrilled to have left poverty
behind, ethnicity, and the small world of the Bronx Jewish ghetto. In leaving behind all that, she had also left behind buying on sale. Her daughters would be raised in
the world of why-pay-less.

After the talk, I gave the heckle more consideration.

Was my mother simply assimilating, or was she an
aspiring WASP? By marrying a WASP (my first marriage), was I furthering the process of assimilation that
she started? Did she subconsciously want me to inter-
marry? Perhaps I gleaned it. Was that the subtext of
"Never buy on sale"?

She also said, "Never eat leftovers." She also said,
"Pick one hairdo and stick to it." She also said, "If a doctor
practices out of town, you have to ask yourself why." She
also said, "You can read anything except the comics." She
abhorred censorship. I was the only kid I knew reading
Peyton Place, a racy sex-filled novel, out in the open.

My mother's rules were our commandments. She was
Moses, and we were her followers. She left Bronx Jewish

behind and established her own religion: Ephron. A sect of writers (which all her daughters eventually became). Services were held nightly at the dinner table. Laughter was the point, not prayer, and the blessing "That's a great line, write it down."

After my divorce, I fell madly in love and married a man who suited me. We were the same religion, and I don't mean Jewish, although Jerry was that. He was a writer, a fellow worshipper of the written word.

After my talk, I mentioned the *farbissina* to people at the Jewish community center where the festival was held. "She's an Israeli," they said, as if that explained everything.

They also said they were probably helpless to do anything about her, as she was a big donor. Obviously they needed her to continue to put bricks in their JCC.

A week later, on my way to a book festival in Atlanta, my friend Joy e-mailed me a link to an article in the *New York Times.* Joy's only comment was "A *shonda.*" (Yiddish for something to be ashamed of.) The article was about the fact that the Marcus Jewish Community Center of Atlanta, host of the festival, had suddenly canceled the appearance of Peter Beinart, a journalist who advocates a liberal take on Zionism and criticizes the established American Jewish community because, to quote the article, it "does not defend democratic values in the Jewish state."

As soon as I arrived, I asked about banning Beinart. The woman driving me was vague. No one knew quite what happened, she told me, only that the head of the book festival was upset and had secured another location for him. The Jewish book festival, however, was not permitted to associate its name with his event. Not permitted? I asked. By whom? She didn't know for sure, but people suspected the community center's big donors. She also said that the book festival was worried that other authors would cancel their festival appearances in protest and solidarity with Mr. Beinart. So far, no one had.

Probably for this reason, I thought: *Those authors want to sell their books.*

I was feeling guilty about being there and trying every which way to justify it. As in, I heard this news too late to cancel. As in, when it comes to Israel, some Jews are irrational, fanatical, or, at the least, not objective. You can't even discuss Israel with them without getting into a BIG ARGUMENT. As in, the author, Peter Beinart, hadn't canceled. He was happy to have another venue. Perhaps he wanted to sell his books, too. He might have even been thrilled because I was told that his new venue sold out immediately. Besides, if he writes about Zionism, he must have an appetite for controversy. I can imagine the tweets and e-mails he gets. Twitter and the online posting of articles is license for anyone not only to comment but to dump rage. A writer can end up the target of a verbal firing squad. The threat of it can censor thoughts before they are written.

I wrote a long guilt-ridden e-mail to my editor, although there was nothing he could advise as I had already "performed" in Atlanta. Ultimately, as the question continued to trouble me, I concluded that I had betrayed my mother and the religion of Ephron, of which one of the commandments was "No censorship."

. . . .

My novel *The Lion Is In*—the one I was discussing/ selling at Jewish books festivals—came from a dream.

Several years before, I had been upset, very upset about illness—my sister Nora and my husband were both sick—and I was thinking, *How in the world am I going to get through this time without heavy-duty drugs?* I went to sleep and had a dream.

There were two women in a bar—well, more a roadhouse than a bar—on a rural highway in North Carolina (a state to which I had never been). Inside the bar, in addition to the women, was a lion. The women were on the lam. I didn't know what they were running from, but I knew that the lion would change their lives.

When I woke up, I had a title, *The Lion Is In*, and I realized that I had dreamed the premise of a book. I began writing immediately, and writing it provided an alternate reality, a place where I was happy to live every day. A refuge. When I was awake I lived there. And writing exhausted me enough that at night I slept easily.

After I had finished a couple of drafts, my girlfriends insisted I had to go to North Carolina. How could I presume to write about a place where I had never been?

I had placed my roadhouse bar in Northampton County, about sixty miles north of a city called Rocky Mount. One of my best friends, who had been there, told me that it was primarily farming—tobacco and soybeans. There were pine forests. The county had been hard hit by the downturn in the economy, especially by the furniture business moving to Mexico. A place that time forgot. Put another way, a timeless place. That seemed right.

With the book largely finished, I visited. I stayed at a DoubleTree Inn in Rocky Mount, and every day I would pick a random destination, some obscure town, a dot on a map in Northampton County, and instruct the GPS to "take back roads."

In my novel, one of my heroines, Rita (the one who has left her preacher husband), wants Marcel the lion to have a tree. Marcel lives caged in the bar and has never had a tree before, although, with Rita's help, he has begun to venture out. One day, when Rita is driving to a store, she passes an open field with a lone oak tree in it. The tree, bare of all foliage, appears to have been struck by lightning. What remains is only this: a trunk and naked limbs. "More a sculpture than a tree," Rita calls it. She convinces some men to dig up the tree, carry it back to the bar where Marcel lives, and replant it near the parking lot.

So I am in North Carolina, following the disembodied GPS voice to a random destination. I pass an open field. There is the tree. A bit scragglier than I had written it, but unmistakable nonetheless.

I screamed.

I was with my niece, whom I scared to death. She was driving. "Pull over." I might have shouted it.

I got out of the car, and, as I stood by the side of the road, shocked and staring, a pickup truck passed by and stopped. The driver asked if everything was okay. "Yes," I said. "I'm looking at the tree."

"That's my friend's tree," he said. "It's an oak tree," which is what I had written. And, in my novel, Marcel doesn't know what to do with the tree when he first meets it, so he simply rubs himself against it.

The man said to me, "The bark is rubbed off because all the goats over there come over and rub themselves against the tree."

When I spoke at the book festivals, I always told this story. I always said, "Isn't this strange?" Or, "Isn't this mystical?" Or, "Isn't this remarkable?" As if I were a teenager recounting some woo-woo moment at a slumber party. Sometimes I likened it to an ESP experience, equivalent to thinking, *I really miss my friend*, and a minute later the phone rings and it's she. Only one woman questioned me further, asking if I thought I'd had a spiritual experience. I said quickly, laughing, "No."

Of course it wasn't some ESP thing or a coincidence. And, as I understand synchronicity (not well), it doesn't appear to be that, either, but something startlingly different, as my friend Joy pointed out one day when I had finished touring.

We are in a café, having cappuccinos and eating *pains au chocolat*. Because we haven't seen each other in a while and are close friends, we are analyzing, pondering, and laughing about absolutely everything. I bring this up. Joy, who is a reporter, Jewish, and more religious than I (but who isn't?), forces the question and points out that I've been avoiding it.

In the dream and in what I wrote as a result, did I invent a higher power, a lion that could solve the problems of not only my heroines' lives but my own, and provide me with comfort and peace? Joy mentions Jacob (in the Old Testament), who dreams of a ladder to heaven. Of course I know nothing of this and don't really see the parallel after a quick Google on my iPhone of the Internet bible, Wikipedia. Nevertheless, how did I write a tree that exists in a place I had never been? How and why did I find it?

"The miracle of Marcel's tree," I say, laughing. No question I am more comfortable with the miracle of surviving a water bug, whose purpose is clear—to provide laughter at the dinner table. My mother's commandments, which I live by, are concrete, pithy. They do not address the mysterious, the intangible, the unknowable. They do not allow for miracles like Marcel's tree.

Have I had some proof, at sixty-six and facing loss, that I am not as alone as I feel? Am I so resistant to this idea that "Marcel" even provided a stranger in a pickup truck to stop, verify it, and offer additional proof?

Joy and I sip our cappuccinos, and the question sits there unanswered. There it will stay.

There is no way I can wrap my brain around this. It requires a leap of faith. A leap of faith conflicts with my religion. It's not that I am "not Jewish enough," but I am too Ephron to ever acknowledge it.

#TheHairReport

I don't care about the weather. I care only what the weather is going to do to my hair. Filling this gap in coverage—surprising, given how much weather reporting there is—I tweet #TheHairReport. I wish it had pictures. The useless weather report on cell phones has pictures. In my hair reports, I imagine round circles (heads) with, depending on the weather that day, straight hair, curly hair, frizzy hair, hair blowing sidewise, flat hair (hat head), long hair flowing in curves (hair with hairography, which, if you're keeping up with hair lingo, you know is the dance in your hair).

Treacherous out. Walk slowly to blow-dry.
Moist. Tendrils expected.

Blizzard coming. Buy shampoo.

Hurricane coming. Sandbag ears.

Hurricane coming. Evacuate extensions.

Prepare for hurricane hair. Make minestrone.

Stay home. Cancel everything.

Bad hair day becomes good one. Sometimes life
   gets better.

Extreme hair happiness. Take it to the streets.

Good hair night. Or good night, hair.

Sunny and mild. Rush to blow-dry. Have
   important photos taken.

Sweat head.

Sweat head continues.

Cold. Sacrifice hair for ears. Wear hat.

Hat head trumps bed head. Root lifter
   recommended.

Tropical. Wash with piña colada.

Bad hair day gets worse. Cover mirrors.

Atlanta. Nice trees, bad hair. Wear leaves.

Charleston. Fried. Like everything else here.

Boston. Fritzy, a notch worse than frizzy.

Rome. Seems like a good place for hair to
   retire to.

Sicily. Hair good. Cappuccino better.

San Francisco. Due to hills, am more worried
   about legs than hair.

Pouring. Take boat to blow-dry.

Put a bow in it. Maybe some tinsel.

Doing the hair tango.

A very good day for hair of all sorts.

Spring. Take your hair for a walk. It doesn't get
   better than this.

Fall. Wear a fall. Don't fall.

Windy. Spray advisory in effect.

Major frizz alert.

Thanksgiving. Outside fine. Inside, beware of
   critical relatives.

Beautiful. A Beyoncé day.

FEAR OF PHOTOS

Many months ago, Julia Gregson and I, best friends and writers, sold an idea for a travel piece to *More* magazine. We had hatched it while having breakfast in my local Pain Quotidien.

Julia and I have been friends for thirty-five years. Our husbands were friends first. Jerry met me and Richard met Julia about the same time, and we all fell in love with one another. They lived in Los Angeles then and moved back to England shortly thereafter, eventually settling in Wales, and we have continued our friendship with extended visits in each other's homes and meeting for vacations. Together we are great travelers. I don't mean to exotic places. To, like, places in Europe. We like to do the same things—walk, talk, and eat. We can spend hours at a café yakking way into the night, wake up the next morning, and fall into another endless conversation at breakfast.

I have recited a poem in French to them (Verlaine). No one can mangle French like me. It may be what I do best. Once we all created a water ballet. In other words, we behave like idiots together. We are always, always, always laughing. Except when we're not, in which case we're always extremely sympathetic.

Julia and I are nothing alike and a perfect match. She is tall. Very tall. About five ten, with auburn hair. Briefly, in her twenties, she was a model, and can still, if pushed, do the model walk with the bored model face. I am shortish—five four—with dark brown hair. My complexion is olive-ish. Hers is whatever goes with redheads, which means she can wear yellow and orange, earth tones, as they say. I am strictly black, navy, and an occasional raspberry (when I can find it, which I never can; it's ridiculous to have mentioned it). Whatever looks good on Julia looks terrible on me. That's how I know what to buy her for her birthday: if it looks bad on me.

Richard and Julia live in a farmhouse (that began as a cowshed in 1330, aka the Middle Ages) on the River Wye with a horse, sheep in the meadow, cavorting lambs in the spring. Their dog got punished recently for eating a farmer's prized chicken (really, it was some sort of valuable chicken beyond, like, being organic). My dog—who walks on a leash on New York City sidewalks and occasionally scarfs a crust of pizza—is terrified of ants. (This is true.)

Julia's e-mails are sometimes about fields of bluebells or horseback rides on frosty hills. Once she rode all the way across Wales on horseback, camping out at night. I occasionally play Ping-Pong. I bowled 154, but when I was thirteen. One day when Julia telephoned (or "rang," as she would say), her husband was out shooting pheasant and mine was playing Word Whomp. When we visit Wales, I miss the subways. Driving where they live is hair-raising, what with the needle-narrow roads and tall hedges and insane roundabouts, not to mention driving in England, where left is right and right is left (and I don't know my left from my right). How incredible that they do it every day.

Julia is also game. She has traveled alone through India and Turkey. She trained wild horses in Australia. She is the person I wish I were.

About four years ago, after a career as a journalist and one novel published, Julia wrote an international bestseller, *East of the Sun*. It's fabulous. I highly recommend it and all of her novels (*Band of Angels* and *Jasmine*

Nights). As they say on Facebook, thumbs up. And by the way, isn't "thumbs up" the biggest cop-out as well as the genius of Facebook? Telling someone you're happy for her in a click. Oh man, does that let you off the hook. I always call Julia and she calls me not only when we need advice and sympathy, but when we have news to celebrate. We are the best kind of friends, truly happy for the good stuff.

So we're sitting in Pain Q having lattes and croissants—one other great thing about Julia, she's never ordering spelt—lamenting the fact that at this time in our lives, we know what we like and repeat it. We live in a comfort zone. Her comfort zone is considerably larger than mine, nevertheless, we should both break out. Shake ourselves up. Grow.

We decide to take a trip together in which we each force/encourage the other to do things we wouldn't normally do, and then write it up in side-by-side diaries. We had to behave, in other words, counterintuitively. Or, as all *Seinfeld* lovers understand, do what George did: order the chicken salad instead of the tuna. Julia suggests we travel to Kenya and work in a rural village. Her daughter Poppy did this on "gap year." In England that's the year between high school and university. One other young woman in Poppy's group was eaten by a crocodile, but

Julia assures me it's very beautiful there. I nix that. I realize I am in over my head. There is nothing Julia is scared of. I am so not in her league.

We forget about it—life happens, as they say—and one day I am having a meeting with some editors at *More* (a magazine for women over, say, thirty-five). They are looking for some travel pieces to assign. I mention this idea. They say, "Great."

We settled on Spain (no crocs). Julia thinks I need to go horseback riding. I had ridden on horseback as a kid at camp in Arizona, but exclusively western saddle, with its large saddle horn to grab on to in case of emergencies. The only time I had tried the sleek, hornless English saddle favored in Spain and by all well-bred equestrians was fifteen years earlier with Julia in Wales. Julia swore that Maggie, my horse, was menopausal. She bolted, taking off into the woods in a wild gallop you get rescued from in a movie by a man you fall in love with. I managed not to fall off, but the trauma remained fresh. Julia thought I needed to face the fear. That was the point of the trip, wasn't it?

I thought we should learn flamenco dancing. It seemed both absurd and sexy, a jolt to our systems. I had some castanets when I was five. My parents brought them back from Mexico, and I was always click-clacking around the house. We agreed we would order strange items off menus, things we had never tasted and were not inclined to. Like salt cod.

I thought I needed to couch surf to get rid of princess tendencies. Couch surfing, if you don't know, is staying in people's homes on their couches or in spare bedrooms. Generally speaking, I prefer vacations where the sheets have a high thread count, the bathroom is full of mini lotions, and a manicure is an elevator floor away. Once Richard and Julia talked us into a walking tour in Cinque Terre. This is such an English thing, walking tours, only it isn't walking, it's hiking. Cinque Terre consists of five little villages nestled together in the mountains on the northwest coast of Italy. If you take a train from one town to the next, it takes five minutes. Maybe three. Through a tunnel. If you walk from one to the next, it takes eight hours up the world's steepest hills and, even worse I discovered, down them. My hips were crying. After the first day, Jerry, Richard, and Julia hiked and I took the train. On the fourth day, in a wisp of a town called Riomaggiore, Jerry and I found ourselves in a hotel room so small, I tripped over myself. Some bugs, too. Outside the window was a stucco wall. I reached out and touched it.

As only a girl raised in Beverly Hills can, I freaked out. I was so freaked, I figured out how to make a call on an Italian pay phone (I don't speak Italian), got an Italian operator (who didn't speak English) to find a hotel in the next town, called the hotel, and booked a reservation and a taxi to take us there. When I knocked on Richard and Julia's door to tell them we were moving on to Porto Venere and would meet them there, they were in their tiny room, happy as can be, lounging on the bed, drinking Prosecco. Admittedly their window did have a view, but still.

To recap the trip: horseback riding, flamenco dancing, couch surfing. And we were going to stay at a monastery for some serious silence (what could be harder?) and spiritual rebooting—or I should say *booting*, as *rebooting* implies that I was at some point spiritual in my past.

No sooner had we settled on this journey, which would take us from Madrid to Seville to Barcelona, than I began to have fantasies of the nightmare variety. I slip on a castanet and end up in traction. I fall off a horse and end up in a coma. My plane will crash and I'll end up dead.

A note about this. Last week I had lunch with a friend who told me that worrying is a depletion of your power. Then someone else told me that worrying is negative goal-setting. Then someone else told me worrying is about having negative expectations. I'm planning to give up worrying. I want to, but I'm worried I won't be able to.

Furthermore, about this trip, I'm almost embarrassed to admit that I had never flown across the Atlantic alone. Everyone I know takes off for parts unknown at the drop of a hat, but travel is not easy for me and never has been. I'm always ambivalent. And by the way, I really have to mention here that the other week I got on a plane for Tulsa, and, just before takeoff—the doors were closed, as they say—the pilot got on the loudspeaker and this is what he said: Something has fallen off the plane. I forget what because it took me by surprise, but the thing that fell off began with an *F*—not a fuselage but like a fin or a flipper. "That's not a problem," the pilot said. "There's a small hole in the plane as a result." I am not quoting exactly, but nearly. "That's not a problem, either," he said. "We just have to fly slowly."

As far as I could tell, no passenger even blinked except me. I said to my husband, "Should we get off?" He shrugged. We went to Tulsa. It took forever to get there, but we did, which, as we all know, is the important thing. I am not a fan of flying.

Nevertheless, I was going to Spain.

Then, a couple of weeks before we were supposed to leave, my editor announced something that should have been obvious from the start. The magazine was planning to send a photographer with us.

Suddenly I wasn't getting on a horse. I was getting on a horse and being photographed doing it. For all I knew, I might need a stepladder to get on a horse. I had even learned a useful sentence: I want a short horse. *Yo quiero un caballo corto.* I had learned another phrase—*una copa de vino, por favor*—so that I could order a glass of wine to recover from my day or perhaps imbibe in the hospital where I was in traction or a coma. Where I would undoubtedly also be photographed.

Being photographed raised all sorts of concerns. Where to get a decent blow-dry in Barcelona, Seville, Madrid, and a monastery. I have short curly hair. Without a blow-dry, I look like a tulip. Hair anxiety. I could not be photographed with bad hair. And what about makeup? I couldn't stop by a department store every morning to see if the Bobbi Brown counter would make me up, which I sometimes do if a photograph is going to end up somewhere public. They don't have makeup counters in monasteries. When I vacation, I never think about makeup or hair. That's the definition of a vacation. Would a photo of me flamenco dancing with bad hair and no makeup end up circling the Web for eternity?

When you get older, and I am older, it is harder to

take a good picture. Sometimes I open my iPad and by accident tap Photo Booth and about pass out. I am not a fan of the candid shot.

I called Julia in a panic. I tried to work her into a frenzy, mentioning the horror of being photographed flamenco dancing. That didn't upset her too much. I carried on about candid shots without blow-dries, which didn't upset her too much, either. Of course her hair isn't half as curly as mine. Also she was once a model. She might not think of the camera as a weapon of destruction. Besides, she has the adventure gene. The adventure gene rules. I pine for it.

Still, being the most loyal, most understanding friend a girl could ask for, she understood. Too much stress.

We canceled.

To this day, I don't really know why I needed to cancel. Was it fear of flying, fear of riding, fear of dancing, or fear of photos? Does vanity trump all?

DOGS

My dog's name is Honey Pansy Cornflower Bernice Mambo Kass.

She has more than one name because, when I was about twenty, I was having a hamburger, fries, and a Coke in a coffee shop near my apartment. I was hanging out with friends, but I was drinking my soda the way I did with my parents—sipping it slowly to make it last the meal. Suddenly it hit me: *I'm on my own. I can have more than one Coke. If I can afford it, I can have two Cokes, and, if I don't care if my teeth rot, three.* This was a pivotal growth moment that somehow led fifteen years later to giving my first dog thirteen names. And my second dog, six. (The second-born's arrival never gets as much attention as the first; that's my sense of it as a second-born myself. The second-born is sweeter, however, at least in the case of my dog.)

At this point it is only fair to say that if you don't have a dog, you might want to skip to the next essay. Talking about one's dog can be as boring as people talking about their grandchildren. Dogs are the dog owners' revenge on grandparents—unless you have a dog and grandchildren, too, in which case you are a double threat in the boredom department. There are apparently some 77 million dog owners in this country, which adds up to a lot of boring talk, a portion of which I am responsible for (much as it pains me to admit it because, in the family I grew up in, being called boring was like being called an ax murderer). I might have that statistic wrong. Perhaps it's 77 million dogs, not dog owners. I can't keep facts straight. Numbers especially. Either way, it's an awesome statistic.

I did not grow up with dogs. For a short time we had two ducks. I or one of my sisters won them at a carnival. They were very cute yellow ducklings and they grew up in a flash to be very large white ducks. (I know it's obscene to have city children win baby farm animals, but that's what happened at the spring carnival at El Rodeo elementary, and, as far as the fifties go, that was the least of it.) They lived in the garage and swam in a small inflatable kiddie pool until they disappeared one night. I have no idea what happened to them. Most likely my parents had a hand in it, or possibly a roving dog, which is what we were told. We didn't mourn them. Also I had two very small turtles, Sunshine and Moonglow (possibly also won at a carnival), and it pains me to confess I let the water dry up in their bowl. In other words, I killed them.

Twelve or so years later, when I was taking a required science class in college, I had to cut a planaria in half. A planaria is a flatworm and, if you cut it in half, it regenerates, grows another head and tail. I cut mine in half, went off to Yale for the weekend, and when I returned my planaria was dead. There was a note from my professor. *I didn't think you were the sort of person to let a planaria die.* But he was wrong. Because of Sunshine and Moonglow, I knew that I was exactly the sort of person to let a planaria die.

I got a dog because my friend Deena got a dog. That's one of the best things about friends. Because they do something, you do something—something wonderful that you would never do. At the time I was married and living in Los Angeles with my two stepchildren. (And just as an aside, if you are a stepparent, rush right out and get yourself a dog. Because it's very nice to have someone in the house that loves you.)

We had Daisy, a rescue, for thirteen years. She was part Tibetan Terrier, which probably means nothing to you, but she had a coat of white and brown fur so soft and beautiful, you could wear it to a ball. She was about twenty-five pounds (not too big, not too small). Truly gorgeous.

Like gorgeous people, she knew she didn't have to work hard to get attention. People on the street fell all over her, drivers shouted out of car windows, "What is she?" "A mutt," I would shout back, knowing I had the most beautiful mutt in the world. Whenever I walked her, she would bark at the wind. This never failed to enchant me. In truth, however, she was a bit of a withholding dog, not one for a cuddle or a kiss.

We lived in Los Angeles longer than we should have because I couldn't bear to put Daisy in the cargo hold of an airplane. Then the Northridge quake happened.

I had never been in a big earthquake. Only a small one where the ground trembled in a soft roll and you might even ask someone, "Was that an earthquake?" and then call a friend and say, "I was just in an earthquake," as if something titillating had happened. When this quake,

6.7 on the Richter scale, struck at 4:31 a.m., we were jolted awake by violent shaking. We lived twenty miles away from the epicenter. Still, it was fearsome.

While we were sitting around in the dark afterward (all the lights had blown) waiting for aftershocks and listening to the relentless blare of car alarms set off by the tremors, I said to my husband, "If I die tomorrow, I want to die in New York." No more "Daisy doesn't get on a plane." She had a tranquilizer and survived. Back she moved with us to New York City and she preferred it as we did if you don't count the time a huge, hideous dog living in the apartment next door tried to murder her in the elevator.

Then she got old and sick and died.

That's what dogs do. They die on you.

Which is why I avoid reading most dog memoirs, because the dog always dies. And I weep buckets, which I did when Daisy died. I wept and wept and wept and wept.

After that I moped over dog adoption websites. Then I compulsively watched *Crossing Over*. This show had a popular run on cable in 2000 or so, around the time I was grieving for Daisy. Psychic John Edward (not to be confused with political John Edwards) stood in front of a live studio audience and connected with their "loved ones" who had "passed."

John Edward really did know remarkable things about people who had passed. About hydrangeas they loved or a miniature Christmas tree in a box, or that a woman met her husband on a tennis court, or that a death was violent, a knife involved. He made peace for everyone, and everyone wanted to see their relatives in the afterlife, which I wouldn't think is true for all people (but was true for anyone who wanted show tickets). Then I started watching *The Pet Psychic* with Sonya Fitzpatrick, an eccentric Englishwoman. Sonya communicated with dogs, cats, birds, primates, pretty much any animal. Lots of them had miserable pasts, tied up, starved, it was heartbreaking. All the dogs were big on wanting their owners to know they were grateful for finally having a happy life. The pets were always saying thank you, thank you, thank you. (Unlike children.) Once, as I recall, sensing a llama wanted to wear her silk scarf, Sonya tied it around the animal's long neck. After they were done communicating, the llama's owner tried to untie the scarf. "She wants to keep it," said Sonya, just as the llama whacked him with her head and knocked him over.

Then there was a psychic summit, which I also watched. John Edward from the Sci-Fi Channel network along with his wife and his two fluffy white dogs went to visit Sonya on Animal Planet. Edward and his wife

wanted to get Sonya to find out why their dogs were peeing and pooping (she called it "whoopsing") indoors. She
didn't get anywhere with that, but she did know that one
of the dogs, Jerily (I think that's his name) always liked
his biscuits broken up into little pieces. Both dogs were
wondering about the floor. It turned out the Edwards
were installing new flooring. The dogs wanted to know if
there would be any carpet, which they preferred. Also a
weird shoe thing came up. One dog asked about "the one
shoe." The Edwards had recently opened a baby present
and instead of two shoes, a pair, there had been only one.
The dog "told" Sonya he wanted the shoe.

What I really want to say about my watching all this
is that having a dog/loving a dog/losing a dog turned me
into a nut.

What a remarkable love it is if I wept buckets and
still wanted another, knowing the new one would die on
me, too. That's possible anyway with anyone—that they
might die first—but with dogs, it's nearly inevitable. Dog
years. They're teenagers, according to my vet, at one and
a half or two. They are simply so glorious when they're
around.

I saw a documentary on television about how adapt-
able dogs are. They've figured out humans and how to
connect with them. Unlike wolves. You can't turn a wolf

into a dog no matter how hard you try, which is a lesson about bad boyfriends. Dogs will be around forever. They will outlive the Catholic Church and the Republican Party, just to name two things in the world that seem unable to adapt. Evolution—something many Catholics and Republicans deny—will ultimately be the end of them.

Honey, a Havanese, was not a rescue, which I feel guilty about, but she is a perfect dog—affectionate, friendly, mostly obedient.

As we were driving up I–95 to Royal Flush Havanese in Charleston, Rhode Island, I read *Dog Training for Dummies*, about how to pick a puppy suitable for an old retired couple, which sounded right to me. And I share. First of all, get a girl. I'm not certain that was in the book, maybe it's simply my prejudice. Second of all, hold the puppy and turn it over on its back. It should resist for a second—its legs will wave around—and then relax (showing that it trusts you). Also the puppy should walk toward you with its tail down, a sign of respect. That means you will dominate the dog and the dog won't dominate you. Honey did all those things, and the other puppies did not. One walked away and the other jumped all over us.

Among other things, having a dog provides a more entertaining form of junk e-mail. Along with being inundated with pleas and requests from Guy Cecil, Joe

Biden, Chuck Schumer, Planned Parenthood, and the American Red Cross, today I got an e-mail inviting Honey to participate in a dog shedding competition. It wasn't about hair. Honey doesn't shed, anyway. It was a dog reality show like *The Biggest Loser.* Shedding meant pounds. Many dogs are overweight, no surprise. Who can resist giving a dog a treat? They fixate. They stare you into submission. Honey, who weighs seventeen pounds, weighs two pounds too much. That is quite a lot. Without telling you my weight, let me put it this way: Honey losing one dog pound is like my losing fourteen. I didn't enroll her, however. Much as I love my dog, she is not a career.

Recently, to see how insane the dog world can be, I went over to the preliminary judging of the super fancy Westminster Dog Show. It took place in the huge warehouses used for exhibition on the Hudson River piers. In addition to rings where you could see the dogs parade around while being judged, a huge portion of the space was given over to dogs being prepared to show. As far as the eye could see were rows of dogs on tiny tables getting blow-dries. The dogs were being brushed, combed, and flat-ironed. Lots of flat-ironing. They were being sauced with whipped cream mousse and styling cream, sprayed with Tresemmé Extra Firm. The fur around their mouths—their doggie beards—was parceled into tiny ponytails, wrapped in cloth and secured with rubber bands, to be certain no eye gunk migrated there, dirtying their faces, turning them into, well, dogs. When the trainers showed the dogs, trotting them around the ring, most had hairbrushes tucked into the back waist of their pants or skirts, and the minute there was a break, the trainer whipped out the brush and gave the dog a sprucing. One other weird thing: While the dogs were awaiting their turns, the trainers frequently bit off a bit of treat in their mouths and gave it to them. In other words, the intimacy was a tad freaky. I hope those treats were actual chicken or cheese, and not yam and venison treats in the form of brown bricks, which is what Honey gets (the only other food she is allowed besides kangaroo).

When I returned home, the second I opened the front door, I heard the thumpety-thump of Honey's paws on the stairs—there is no sweeter sound—and then she appeared looking like a dirty shag rug in someone's garage. Show dogs have as much in common with dogs as dolled-up little girls in pageants do with little girls.

When Honey was about five, we had a pet psychic over, who charged quite a bit, at least as much as one month's telephone bill. The ostensible reason for this visit was that I had written a screenplay about a pet psychic and wanted to meet one.

Just as an aside I want to tell you about this screen-play, *Sammy*, because it's one of my favorites and it never got made. The setup: a woman who talks to animals falls in love with a man who talks to the dead. Only thing is, she can actually do it and he can't. Because he's a fraud, he thinks she's a fraud. Because she's for real, she thinks he's for real. The man has a dog, Sammy. The dog falls in love with the woman and rats him out. As I mentioned, it never got made, but at least, because I have included it here, it exists, albeit briefly.

My friend Carol recommended Jocelyn the pet psychic. Jocelyn had met Carol's dog, Dainty, and told Carol why Dainty didn't want to pee on a certain patch of grass but would be happier peeing on another patch. This turned out to be absolutely true and solved a BIG PROBLEM. Jocelyn, a lovely woman in her, I'm guessing, late thirties, was not peculiar in any way except, of course, she could communicate with dogs.

Honey liked her immediately, but Honey likes everyone except really tall people. Whenever anyone new comes over, Honey dances on her hind legs. Isn't that remarkable? Jocelyn immediately pronounced Honey a happy dog with no traumatic past, which we knew. She sat on the rug and observed Honey. After I mentioned Honey's incredible attachment to one of her squeaky toys, a gorilla, Jocelyn said that Honey didn't mind that she wasn't a mother, but she did want a litter of squeaky toy gorillas. Then Jocelyn said to me, "Honey is worried about your left thigh."

The week before, I had had a little growth taken off my left thigh, which turned out to be benign. There was a Band-Aid on the tiny wound, all hidden under my jeans. There was no way Jocelyn could have known about it.

This was startling. And not just because there was no way Jocelyn could have known about it. As irresistible as Honey is and as vulnerable (she trembles in a rainstorm), I have never thought of her as a dog that would run for help if I slipped in a shower or fell through, say, thin ice on a skating pond. I would guess she'd be thinking, *Is it time for lunch, and why aren't you giving it to me?* But apparently not. Apparently I have a really sensitive dog.

Because of the left thigh business, we took Jocelyn seriously and got Honey five more squeaky toy gorillas. They were hard to find online because it turned out they weren't gorillas, they were chimps. (We know the difference between a gorilla and a chimp, but when it comes to squeaky toys, it's hard to tell.) They continue to be the only squeaky toys she likes. She seems to know they are all alike and different from her other toys. Isn't that remarkable?

Honey's tricks: She can burrow under the covers and lie there like a lump.

That's about it.

Except one Sunday last winter, an amazing thing happened. Actually it started the Sunday before. I was making buttermilk pancakes, which I always do on Sunday mornings, and when I put butter on the griddle and turned on the burner, the griddle got so smoky it set off the smoke alarm. Honey went crazy—the piercing sound was painful to her sensitive doggie hearing. She tried to climb my legs. I picked her up and carried her out, and she clung, her little paws digging into my shoulder. The next Sunday, seven whole days later—are you following this?—I took out the griddle, put on some butter, turned on the burner, and Honey tried to climb my legs.

She must have associated the burner with the shriek of the alarm. Or the butter with the shriek, or the pancake griddle with it. The first week the alarm went off at least three minutes after the burner was lit and the butter melted. The second time, the alarm never went off. Still she made the connection.

Isn't she brilliant?

Now you can tell me all about your grandchildren. Or your cat.

IF MY DAD
COULD TWEET

My dad can't tweet because he's dead. He died in 1992, when telephones were still about the only way to have a conversation with someone who wasn't in the same place you were.

My dad was an uproar man. Uproar was his specialty. He loved calling one daughter with news of another, often inaccurate, trying to stir up trouble and envy. When he was close to death and could barely recognize his own hands, he still remembered my telephone number and continued to call any hour of the day or night. There was no caller ID then. I didn't have the option of knowing who it was and not answering.

"Hello," I would say.

"Your sister won the Pulitzer," he would say. And hang up.

As I said, he never got it right. Or perhaps he was simply ahead of the story.

When Ashton Kutcher unleashed an avalanche of Twitter hysteria with his tweet, "how do you fire Jo Pa? #insult #noclass as a hawkeye fan I find it in poor taste" (Kutcher was apparently unaware that Joe Paterno, Penn State head coach, was fired for covering up a child sex abuse scandal) . . . and then Alec Baldwin threw a Twitter tantrum because an American Airlines flight attendant told him it was time for takeoff, he had to stop playing Words with Friends . . . I realized how much my dad would have loved to tweet.

He would have instantly grasped its possibilities. How enormously it magnifies the opportunity for attention and family embarrassment. Like Baldwin and Kutcher, my dad was a Hollywood guy, a screenwriter and producer. His calls, much like their tweets, were variations on a theme: *I'm still here, look at me, ignore me at your peril.*

He never would have mastered the finer points of tweeting. The retweet, the Follow Friday, the hashtag, the @—all the ways one tweeter can communicate with another. My father would have preferred the basic no-frills tweet because he wouldn't have to have a conversation. Which required paying attention to what the other person was saying. Which was a bother. My dad could be sweet, but listening was not his strong suit. On his phone calls (so memorable that I and my sisters Nora and Amy have written about them, and I have no doubt that Hallie will, too), he never said hello or good-bye, those polite fronts and backs that Twitter disposes of anyway. His calls were short blasts. The 140-character restriction was made for him. Like the uproar tweeters of today, he always acted innocent after causing trouble, affecting a kind of how-did-this-happen mode when he'd engineered it.

But mostly he was into bragging. When I think of the calls I've missed about his Twittering:

"I've got two thousand followers."

"I've got ten thousand followers."

"Hey, your old man's got more followers than God."

"Baby, guess who shut down the system?"

My father was crushed when Hollywood lost interest in him. When he couldn't get work. When no one knew his name. But men like my father will be able to prolong their fame, thanks to cyberspace, long after they can't get jobs in television or the movies. If Twitter shuts you down, there's always Facebook, which Salman Rushdie used to blow off a girlfriend. A man with a need for uproar always finds an opportunity.

Once when I complained to my dad about his calls, which came one after another exactly as tweets do, in a relentless, endless stream, he said by way of an apology, "I live half my life in the real world and half on the telephone."

He was truly ahead of his time.

BAKERIES

My favorite thing is a bakery, and my favorite thing about where I live is how many bakeries are a dog's walk away. Dogs aren't allowed in bakeries, but many Manhattan bakeries have little benches in front so you can tie your dog's leash to a bench leg and keep watch out the window to make sure your dog isn't dognapped while you are buying a croissant.

If I head to the West Village, I stop at Bien Cuit for a hockey puck–shaped thing with raisins and I think a hint of orange. I don't have a discerning palate. "It tastes good" is as discerning as I get. This hockey puck is called a granola cookie. Granola cookies are popping up everywhere. I'm pro anything new bakerywise, especially something

that fools you into thinking it's healthy. I consider a peanut butter cookie a source of protein.

In addition to being pro-bakeries, I am pro-sugar. All
my teeth already have fillings, and whatever else is wrong
with sugar I don't care. Everything in moderation, as they
say, although my attachment to bakeries does not fall into
that category.

There is a famous Danish at Bien Cuit. By famous I
mean it's been in a magazine as one of the best Danish
pastries in New York City. (I love it that our culture is so
shallow that even a Danish can be famous.) This Danish
contains yam, and I'm not wild about it, but I don't really
like pumpkin pie, either. After (or instead of) Bien Cuit,
I visit Amy's Bread on Bleecker Street for a ham, pickle,
and butter sandwich on a baguette and a slice of layer
cake. American layer cake is a great invention and, if you
consider the variations, as remarkable as jazz. From there
I'm off to the Blue Ribbon Bakery, where I am very attached to their pizza bread with sea salt, and my husband
loves their olive bread. Also they have good hummus, but
that's another story, a healthy one, and they make my favorite open-faced sandwich: roasted tomatoes, arugula,
and a special lemony olive oil on their toasted white.

Perhaps rather than go west, I head south through
Washington Square Park, an especially lovely stroll in

spring when the pear trees bloom feathery white, stopping at Mille-Feuille on LaGuardia Place for an excellent latte and a *pain au chocolat* or perhaps for their little round chocolate cookies that are not too sweet. Then maybe I turn east to Balthazar, although there is no way to keep an eye on the dog there. Balthazar has great chocolate chip cookies if you like fat ones with walnuts (they freeze well, too—to defrost, stick them in a toaster oven at 450 for five minutes), and they used to have a pistachio doughnut. It was a terrible cruelty to sell something so delicious and then stop. But I don't want to complain. I am lucky to live in carb paradise and I am lucky to be afflicted with a syndrome (disorder?) that my husband calls Discardia—the tendency to throw things away after a few bites unless I fall in love or am really hungry. Thank God for Discardia, or I would be someone who had to be removed from my house with a crane.

If I walk north, I pass Breads Bakery. I am presently eating my way through the shelves and to date have tasted the almond croissant, the regular croissant, the challah (off the charts, only on Fridays), the babka (too chocolaty for me, but everyone else is bananas for it), the walnut bread (highly recommended), the pain au raisin, and the seven-grain bread (not dense enough). Oh yes, I've tried the chocolate chip cookie (just okay). Then I head up to Spoon for their perfect chocolate brownie, which I take home and eat the tiniest sliver of now and then.

I haven't mentioned any lemon sweets, and lemon is my favorite flavor. I wish someone in the Village would make a great lemon meringue pie. But I don't want to complain.

I have been thinking about bakeries a lot recently as well as about complaining, not simply because I am obsessed with bakeries but because I was reading yet another spate of articles about having it all. Women claiming it's possible to have it all, women claiming they can't have it all, at least one man chiming in, *Hey, what about me, I don't have it all, either.* Sheryl Sandberg, COO of Facebook, is touring the country, teaching women to "lean in." I'm glad she is—women need to be as assertive as possible. We still have miles to go in the equality department, but Sandberg, too, smart as she is about it, has thrown her hat into the having-it-all fray. She falls into the hard-but-possible category, and is the current guru in negotiating this imperfect paradise. With her enviable job, helpful husband, two children (not to mention her bestseller), right now she is Queen Have-It-All.

A while ago a woman named Anne-Marie Slaughter wrote a piece in the *Atlantic* about how she realized that she couldn't have it all. Every so often she surfaces, writing another article or making another round of talk shows on the subject. Slaughter had a dream job in Washington, DC (director of policy planning at the State Department), and a husband and children in Princeton, New Jersey. The setup, she was surprised to discover, nearly derailed her kids. It's hard to imagine someone as highly educated as Slaughter not knowing that, if you have kids, it's best to live in the same city they do. If you have a husband, it's a good thing to hang around him, too. Her problem wasn't trying to have it all and realizing she couldn't. It was wanting something so much that she ignored the obvious.

Every choice makes some things in life more possible and some things less—remember upsides and downsides? Actually there is a statistical theory, degrees of freedom, that proves that every single choice you make narrows your choices (the choices you might make in the future), rendering having it all impossible. I dropped out of Advanced Algebra (even though algebra has nothing to do with this, it gives you an idea of my mathematical limits), nevertheless, I will attempt to explain. Take Anthony Weiner, for instance. As I write this, he is all over the news, trying to make a comeback. Anthony Weiner discovered that he could not be a United States congressman and tweet a picture of his erect penis. Becoming a congressman—convincing us to vote for him—ruled out that possibility. He could not have it all. And he's a man.

I'm sure when Anthony Weiner found out he couldn't have it all, he changed the definition. "Having it all" meant having his pregnant wife not leave him. "That's all I want," I bet he said to himself when he was exposed and had to resign. "Just don't let Huma leave me." He might even have said a prayer to that effect if he's the praying type, or even if he's not (circumstances can turn a non-prayer into a prayer). In other words, "all" shrank. However, now that he's got his wife and his baby son—she didn't leave him—"all" is not enough. He wants more. He wants to be mayor. Of New York City. He wants to have the public get past his tweeting his erect penis, have a wife, son, and be mayor, too.

Having it all seems to breed wanting more. And since we can't have it all because it is statistically impossible, and since there is no such thing as more than all, the whole notion seems, I'm sorry to say, depressingly American.

In Ethiopia, 2 percent of women know how to read. The other day the front page of the newspaper featured a story of an eleven-year-old Afghani girl sold into marriage to pay her father's debt. In the photo she was sitting on a chair, wearing a pretty flowing red head scarf. She looked so young and innocent that she might at any second bounce up and do an unselfconscious twirl. In many countries, having it all is learning to read. Having it all is getting to choose who you love. Having it all is walking to school without worrying that you might get raped on the way.

One of the most revolting parts of the American female version—and there are many revolting parts—is that having it all defines "all" one way: marriage, children, career. It assumes all women want the same thing. Success rests on achieving three goals (life viewed not as a continuum, but an endpoint), and these goals, as it happens, are exactly the ones that will declare you a success at your high school reunion.

This might not be a coincidence.

Never underestimate the power of high school. It's the identity everyone wants to live down, the approval everyone aspires to. Being able to check the boxes—marriage, children, career—is more important at a high school reunion than anywhere else, which is why I think that high school, not feminism, is the reason an idea of happiness got framed this way. It instantly creates the social world of high school: haves, have-nots, wannabes, and freaks. Freaks are those who aspire to other versions of life, who want to march to their own tune. Thanks to this definition of success, they will always be freaks. Freaks forever.

And what if you're too poor to have it all? Ironically, you have it all—marriage, children, career—but only because it's a necessity. You have to work to help support your family. Then you are in the impossible state of having it all and having nothing. It's like you have the jeans, but the wrong brand. What a loser. You never get it right.

My friend Molly graduated from high school in 2003, just before Facebook was founded, and as a result, she says, she has never left high school. She keeps bumping into her classmates on Facebook, even those she hasn't spoken to since high school. Daily she is bombarded by photos and news of the have-it-alls. She keeps redefining what she wants, she says, by seeing what everyone else has.

Getting away from high school is supposed to free you from the pressure to conform. But now that there's no getting away, high school is forever. Perhaps Sheryl Sandberg is not Queen Have-It-All. She is Prom Queen Have-It-All.

To me, having it all—if one wants to define it at all—is the magical time when what you want and what you have match up. Like an eclipse. A perfect eclipse is when the moon is at its perigee, the Earth is farthest from the sun, and when the sun is observed near zenith. I have no idea what that means. I got the description off a science website, but one thing is clear: It's rare. This eclipse never lasts more than seven minutes.

Personally, I believe having it all can last longer than that. It might be a fleeting moment—drinking a cup of coffee on a Sunday morning when the light is especially bright. It might also be a few undisturbed hours with a novel I'm in love with, a three-hour lunch with my best friend, reading *Goodnight Moon* to a child, watching a Nadal-Federer match. Having it all definitely involves an ability to seize the moment, especially when it comes to sports. It can be eating in bed when you're living on your own for the first time or the first weeks of a new job when everything is new, uncertain, and a bit scary. It's when all your senses are engaged. It's when you feel at peace with someone you love. And that isn't often. Loving someone and being at peace with him (or her) are two different things. Having it all are moments in life when you suspend judgment. It's when I attain that elusive thing called peace of mind.

Not particularly American, unquantifiable, unidentifiable, different for everyone, but you know it when you have it.

Which is why I love bakeries. Peace descends the second I enter, the second I smell the intoxicating aroma of fresh bread, see apricot cookies with scalloped edges, chocolate dreams, cinnamon and raisin concoctions, flights of a baker's imagination, and I know I am the luckiest person in the world. At that moment, in spite of statistical proof that this is not possible, I have it all. And not only that, I can have more.

UPGRADE HELL

Recently I heard that Twitter redesigned its bird. The logo. The little bird.

I have only recently mastered the language of Twitter—well, most of it. There are still a few symbols I'm clueless about. And I'm worried. Is Twitter going to do to me what Facebook has done?

I'm referring to the Timeline. Although by the time you've read this, for all I know the Timeline may be ancient history. For reasons that will make sense only to Facebook and will probably benefit only Facebook (and the advertisers they are pining for), they will have decided their "users" need a change. They will announce that Facebook has been—this word I am terrified of—upgraded.

In the beginning, the Facebook page was basic. Even a moron (me) could understand it. At the top of the page you posted a message. Below that, "friends" could respond, and below that were your earlier posts. Now, thanks to this newer, better thing called a Timeline—I'm sure many people, younger people, understand why it's called this, but I don't—there are multiple columns. The Facebook page is now completely confusing. What is new? What is old? The messages are where? Where? Your eye is flying around having no idea where to land.

Microsoft Word "improves" itself constantly. I just got a new computer and was forced into a $149 upgrade. I also had to spend $199 on a new version of Final Draft, the software program that screenwriters use. "Don't get Eight, whatever you do, it's worse than Seven," I was warned by screenwriter friends. Final Draft 7 is so preferred that the other week I found one for sale on eBay for $400.

Upgrades are rarely better or easier. In the previous version of Word, if you wanted to do something simple like use boldface or italics or perhaps center a paragraph, the options stretched across the top of your screen in a friendly here-I-am-click-on-me kind of way. In the current version, everything is hidden (as it also is in the recently revamped Gmail). One is helpless in the face of technology marching needlessly on. Where is boldface? Italics? Hello? After endless searching—and it is risky to click on anything unknown on a computer because you can end up in a cyber world you can't escape from, then you will have to call tech support and that will surely wreck your day—after clicking willy-nilly, I found, under View, something called "Formatting Palette." Palette? I'm not a painter, but hey, I clicked on it and up popped a small box with all the options—boldface, italics, font size, etc.—crammed into it. I practically needed a magnifying glass to use it. And would I remember where it was when I needed it next?

The television show *Are You Smarter Than a 5th Grader?* proves that adults often aren't. When it comes to upgrades, they surely are not. A fifth grader who's been using a computer, as many have, since kindergarten could have found boldface in ten seconds.

Baby boomers cannot keep learning new things, stuffing new information into their overcrowded brains. We're already passing out from it. We're being upgraded into obsolescence.

I don't want more options. I want fewer options. There are sixty buttons on my remote control, and I have used twelve of them. Sometimes I hit the wrong button and a tiny screen pops up in the corner of my big one and I can't get rid of it.

Actually, in fact, I have three remote controls, and I have been told several times that I can have them consolidated into one remote control. I dread everything about this—buying the remote, hiring a techie genius or begging a fifth grader to explain how to use it, and then immediately forgetting how approximately one second after he leaves my apartment.

Which brings me to *Law & Order*, arguably the most successful television franchise ever. *Law & Order*, in reruns at almost every hour of the day or night, is as relentlessly repetitive as a metronome. Every episode begins the same way—a body is found. This discovery is followed by a few ominous musical beats, the same ominous musical beats every episode. Two detectives go from place to place. We know that because each place is announced with the same musical cue, plus words on the screen tell us exactly where they are. Or I should say, more important, the words tell us exactly where *we* are. At between twenty-seven and twenty-nine minutes past the hour, a bad guy is arrested and the show switches from law to order.

When Dick Wolf, the creator, spun out other versions,

such as *Law & Order: SVU*, he kept the format virtually the same. Only the nature of the crimes changed. In this chaotic world of constant upgrades, where I can't even find boldface, I am so grateful to him. All I want is for someone not to change something I love. All I want is for someone to keep it simple.

Recently Apple unveiled a new iPhone with two hundred more features. Facebook announced that it was going to develop a smartphone. My phone is already too smart for me, and I assume this new phone will be smarter. All a smarter phone means is another way for me to feel dumber.

YOUR ORDER HAS
BEEN SHIPPED

A few days ago, I got an e-mail from my sister Amy in Los Angeles saying she and her husband had received boxes from J.Crew. Christmas presents from me, she assumed, since I had ordered them online and told her to expect them.

But for whom? she asked. The cards were buried deep in the packaging, and one of them was missing. Nothing was gift wrapped, either (although I had requested and paid for it). The boxes contained two pairs of shoes (although I had ordered only one pair), a man's pullover, and a sparkly pink woman's sweater. The sweater was for a friend who also lives in Los Angeles, but somehow ended up being sent to Amy's husband.

I called J.Crew to complain, and what followed was tedious and time-consuming, as all Internet dramas are, involving a review of numerous e-mails—"your order has been received," "your order has been shipped"—in this case to the wrong place and in the wrong ways, some of which I might have prevented if I'd been vigilant tracking the flurry of e-mails.

The customer service representative, consulting records, assured me that the box for my friend had been delivered. It had been left at the front door, she said, and gave me the address, which turned out to be not my sister and her husband's house but my friend's office, a gigantic building in Beverly Hills. "Left outside the front door? Are you sure?"

"Yes," she said, and, as an apology, she would send me a $50 gift card. I e-mailed my friend. Had she received a box from J.Crew? "No," she said.

My sister offered to gift wrap and deliver my friend's present. This was especially kind because traffic in Los Angeles is awful, as bad as New York's during the holidays, which is one reason I order on the Web. But rather than make life easier, Web shopping only complicates it in new, more frustrating ways.

My husband, in charge of buying for all the children in our life, announced one evening that he had bought all his presents. To be done with Christmas shopping was so exciting that you'd think he'd used up some calories to do it, when in fact he'd never left his desk. The next morning he got an e-mail from Hammacher Schlemmer saying the item was out of stock and would ship after January 1. So he had to phone and cancel the order. He then had to Web-shop all over again.

When I ordered the presents on the J.Crew website and checked a box for gift wrapping, I received a message back that J.Crew did not wrap shoes, my sister's present. As Amy and I were sorting things out, I wondered why in the world I thought it was okay to send a Christmas present that wasn't gift wrapped.

It seems to me—a fact I had completely forgotten—that a Christmas present should be wrapped in pretty paper, maybe with some Santas dancing across it, maybe something glossy and glamorous. Shouldn't the tag be handwritten? Shouldn't the ribbon be made of paper that curls when you whip it across a scissor blade? A present should beckon you. Who wants a Christmas tree with a bunch of UPS boxes under it?

Last week a UPS box arrived. I opened it, and inside, unwrapped, was a slate cheese board and a gift card that said, in computer script, *Merry Christmas Julia and Jerry, love Anna.*

Anna is my niece. Jerry is my husband. I assume that I am Julia.

Precious holiday giving cannot be entrusted to a website. A gift shouldn't be something you open by accident—*Hello, what is this?*—ripping open the cardboard outer box with a knife and then having your present fall out naked.

Ordering Christmas presents on the Web, regardless of the dubious ease, has obliterated the idea that there should be some grace to a present, some beauty, and that the receiver should experience it. Instead it's become as mundane and problematic as all our Web purchases, which in my family include paper towels and toilet paper.

All this joy of Internet shopping was accompanied by our phone ringing several times a day: a computer voice from Virgin America insisting that my husband owes $70—a $50 credit card fee and $20 interest for not paying it. My husband has never had a Virgin America credit card. But to "proceed," as in clear the problem up, the electronic voice asked him to identify himself by giving the number of the credit card that he does not possess. The telephone, which used to symbolize "reach out and touch someone"—remember that tear-jerking TV ad?—has become a disembodied voice reaching out to drive us crazy.

But I digress. Or do I? It all seems related. Intimacy replaced by expedience.

So this is my New Year's resolution: I am never ordering another Christmas present on the Web again. Next year I am wrapping all my gifts myself and standing in line at the local post office for an hour or two to mail them. It's the least I can do for the people I love.

WHY I CAN'T
WRITE ABOUT
MY MOTHER

In the hospital, when she was dying, my mother famously said to my sister Nora, "Take notes." By famously I mean, famous in my family. The statement was embraced as words to live by, written about by all the sisters, considered permission to write anything and everything as well as evidence of what a clear-eyed, original woman my mother—so ahead of her time (screenwriter, career woman, feminist)—was to the end.

"Take notes" is a ruthless deathbed directive, cold and unsentimental. Imagine it. I mean really imagine it. You are lying in your hospital bed, stomach distended from cirrhosis, nearing the end after years of dedicated drinking, of bender upon bender. The alcohol has now not only destroyed your liver but addled your brain. You are facing an imminent all-systems failure, and what do you say to your daughter? "Take notes."

Imagine all the conversations a mother on her death-bed might want to have with her daughter, all the possible affections that might be tendered. Imagine what you might say to your own daughter. And then think, *This is what she said.*

Perhaps she knew we wouldn't be crying and was providing an alternative. Something to keep us busy while we weren't grieving. That presumes a consideration she wasn't known for—an awareness of our needs. Dependence on alcohol, the illness of alcoholism, sadly breeds a staggering self-absorption. Grieving might have been something she couldn't wrap her brain around. One other thing about drinking—it blots feeling, numbs pain. Allows you to travel or stumble around in an anesthetic haze. Feelings were the opposite of a comfort zone for my mother. "Take notes." At the time she said this, she hadn't had a sober day in years. Still we found wisdom in it. Our brilliant mother. We kept her on the pedestal in spite of evidence to the contrary. Dropped what didn't fit the myth out of the equation. "Take notes" might be helpful. It is certainly clever, and cleverness, highly valued in my family, was sometimes mistaken for or confused with wisdom. It is for sure a distancing mechanism: *Don't be with me, take notes on me.* As I said, feelings were not my mother's strong suit. She had worked her way around that problem by distilling into pithy rules a remarkable amount of useful information about living an interesting nonconformist writer's life.

Was she aware, when she was dying, that there was no way for us to miss her? To admire her, yes. To be grateful for her, yes. To be sad for her because she drank her life away, yes. To be relieved, yes. To miss her, no.

But wait. Let me start over.

All siblings have different parents. We are all born at different times in our parents' marriage. Parents do not treat their children identically, much as they might imagine they do or strive to, and children bond or not and relate differently to each parent. This is obvious, but it is important to state because, in spite of having three sisters, this is my story, only my story, and the sister to whom my mother said "Take notes" was not me. When I wrote in an earlier paragraph that there was no way to miss my mother and used the pronoun *us*, I misspoke. I was referring only to myself.

So let me begin differently.

When I was about fourteen years old, I was hanging

out after school at home in the sunroom. The sunroom was my favorite room, friendly Southern California casual. Glass walls on two sides hung with thick straw shades, straw sisal on the floor, although I don't think it was called sisal then, so let's just say a carpet made of straw. I was slouched on one of the bamboo couches with my feet up on the coffee table, reading while I watched television. This is what I did almost every day after school, and most likely there was a pile of chocolate chip cookies on my lap and I was eating the cookie part first and saving the chips for last. The sunroom was two steps down from the dining room, and I became aware of my mother at the top of the steps looking down at me.

"I hope you never tell anyone what happens here," she said.

Did I nod back? I certainly quickly agreed. This was not an invitation to a conversation, and I was always wary around my mother. She was unpredictable. She could be mean. What she was referring to—"what happens here"— were the drunken brawls and raging fights between my parents that happened at night. Not every night. But often.

During the day things were fairly normal. They got tense around dinnertime, sixish, when the first glasses of Scotch on the rocks were poured. I was always trying to read the signs, the looks between them, jerky movements: Were they angry? What was coming? Would tonight be one of those nights? Should I finish my homework early just in case? (I was very responsible, as children of alcoholics often are.)

I might be getting ahead of the story. Life is such a jumble. Especially looking back.

"I hope you never tell anyone what happens here" was a reference to the nights made during the day. These are, I should point out, the things that children of alcoholics are sensitive to. Minutiae. Subtle details. Meanings that might sail over another child's head. I was always decoding. I was hyperalert.

Being hyperalert is a lasting thing. Being a watcher. Noticing emotional shifts, infinitesimally small tremors that flit over another person's face, the jab in a seemingly innocuous word, the quickening in a walk, an abrupt gesture—the way, say, a jacket is tossed over a chair.

"I hope you never tell anyone what happens here." This was important. This was an acknowledgment in the day that the nights existed. My mother was admitting this. Startling, really. She never had before.

So: "Take notes" and "I hope you never tell anyone what happens here." Mixed messages.

Or simply different thoughts at different times?

Or, looked at another way, perhaps Nora was supposed to "take notes" and I was supposed to keep my
mouth shut. Perhaps my mother knew which of us was
Judas.

So let me begin again.

When my mother was dying, I went to visit her in the
hospital. I was about to have my first book published—
The Adventurous Crocheter, a craft book about crocheting. (This is an important fact—please remember it.)

I hadn't seen my mother in some months; I was living
in Rhode Island. She was so thin as to be nearly unrecog-
nizable, and, weirdly, as a result I saw our physical re-
semblance for the first time, because my face is thin and
now hers was too. I had never felt mothered by her, but I
could see clearly that she was my mother. I was twenty-
seven, unhappily married, and for the most part without emotional support. My mother and I weren't close and
never had been. If only. Then I could have simply said
what was in my heart or trusted that my heart would show
the way. At least that's what I have always imagined, the
way mothers and daughters might relate when alcohol is
not part of the equation.

Oh, God, let me begin again, because what is really
driving me crazy is this: My mother wasn't funny. I wish
she had been funny. I don't mean that she never said

anything funny. I don't remember that she did, but she must have because she wrote funny things in her plays and movies.

For me everyone is much easier to write if I can find the comedy in their natures. Comic characters are lovable simply because they are funny. Even if they drive you nuts, seriously nuts, if you can write them funny, the love shows through. This is why I was able to write a comic novel (*Hanging Up*) based on my dysfunctional (*disturbed* wouldn't be off the mark, either) relationship with my dad.

In fiction and nonfiction I have mostly steered clear of my mother. This conundrum, how to make her funny, may be entirely self-serving, because if a writer can make someone lovable, then the writer is lovable. The reader assumes it. I think. So I have to give that up.

Wanting to be liked can get in the way of truth. Which is essential.

Anyway, my mother was lying in her hospital bed, and I reminded her of a story she often told at the dinner table when I was young and family dinners were fun. My mother had graduated from Hunter College in New York City. At Hunter all students were required to pass a swimming test, and many had never learned to swim. My mother would show up at the pool in a swimsuit with a swim cap on her head, sign in as someone else, and take their test. In return, she always told us, her classmates took her math exams, because she hated math.

I don't know why this tale was told time and time again. Why it was a favorite. It's a story about cheating, but we all found it charming. I have no idea why I fished it out of my brainpan at that particular moment. Small talk on a deathbed. I reminded her of the story, and she said to me, "I didn't hate math. I hated crocheting."

I know the alcohol had pickled her brain. Still, that is what she said. That and not something else.

So last words: "Take notes" to one daughter. "I hated crocheting" to another.

That is actually sort of funny.

My mother was an alcoholic. For me that's where it begins.

She began drinking when I was eleven years old. There was a clear before and after in my life—a sunny before and a dark after. Day/night. Now that I am grateful for the life I have, I think of eleven as a sweet spot— an emotional place that allows me to venture in both directions creatively. In retrospect, eleven is a lot of good years.

I believe having an alcoholic parent is not only something to write about, but that there is an obligation to do it. Growing up as that child is lonely, isolating, confusing, and damaging. There are lots of us. If I have the power by telling a story to make an isolated person less alone, that is a good thing. Besides, I don't believe in protecting parents who drink—sympathizing, forgiving, but not protecting. "I hope you never tell anyone what happens here." Tell everyone. You might never get past it otherwise. The obligation of a child is not to protect their parents. Obviously. Obviously. A mom is supposed to protect her kids. Which doesn't happen when she drinks.

My mother was an alcoholic before anyone knew much about the disease. Before half the world was sober and the other half related to someone who is or should be. Before AA appeared to have more members than the Democratic Party. Before AA was a place to network. Before people were giving up vices willy-nilly—like cigarettes, carbs, or caffeine. Before people gave up sugar (that is, people who didn't have diabetes). Before "giving up" proliferated into a national pastime. Before enlightenment.

I say this because environment matters. AA existed, but was not ubiquitous. My mother died in 1971. First Lady Betty Ford, who sensitized the public to the illness of addiction, didn't confess hers until 1978. When I was young there was barely any information or support for either my mother or me (Al-Anon was founded when I was thirteen, but I had never heard of it). But even with all the knowledge we have today, children are still keeping the secrets their parents want them to keep. Children are loyal.

My bedroom and my mom's bedroom shared a wall. (My parents did not sleep in the same room.) Late at night I could hear my mother's demented drunken ramblings. Who was she angry at—my father, her father? I couldn't make sense of it. She was the lunatic wife locked in the attic in *Jane Eyre*, only she wasn't locked in the attic. She was on the loose. I would put my fingers in my ears, bury my head in the pillow. Nothing shut it out. I would hear her door open and she would pad down to my father's room and the fighting would begin. They would travel all over the house during these vicious shouting matches, sometimes banging open my door and scaring me out of my wits.

"I hope you never tell anyone what happens here."

She spoke in an even tone. She wasn't pleading. She never apologized. If she had weepy morning-after regrets, I wasn't aware of it.

My mother had created a version of herself that she sold to the world: She was completely pulled together. She was a successful career woman. She and my dad wrote movies together, light comedies and musical comedies. Some of these were *Daddy Long Legs* (Fred Astaire and Leslie Caron), *The Jackpot* (Jimmy Stewart), and *There's No Business Like Show Business* (starring, among others, Marilyn Monroe). She had no time for the stuff of ordinary women (we had a cook and nurse for that). Superiority was part of her identity. She didn't meet our teachers—I'm not complaining about that. I was proud that she didn't. "Your mother is too busy to go to open school night," she told us. "She has a career." Having a mother like this set me apart and gave me cachet. Her expectation that I would be a career woman, too, gave me a destiny that other girls didn't have.

"Elope" was something she told me often. This is really odd—what mother doesn't want to see her daughter's wedding? Lesser mothers. Mothers without bigger things on their minds. She never did girlfriend things, not with me, not with girlfriends: shopping, lunches. She didn't have close friends. She had a life without close friends. That breaks my heart. The phone rarely rang for her.

Once she took me shopping. To buy a dress for the first day of first grade, which means I was six. In a small children's store on Wilshire Boulevard. There was another girl trying on a dress with pineapples on it. A pineapple print dress. Tropical, I suppose. I remember having

to summon up the nerve—I must always have been inti-
mated by my mother, because otherwise why would I
remember that this took nerve? I pointed to the dress.
"Could I try that?" My mother said, "I'm not buying you a
dress with pineapples on it."

I don't think she was being mean. I think she was
being funny. Maybe she was funny. That line made it into
Love, Loss, and What I Wore (the play that Nora and I
wrote) in the section called "What My Mother Said," but
we cut it before the play opened because it never got a
laugh. So maybe my mother wasn't funny.

That outing is my first memory of my mother. And
my only memory of us together. But she did not have children and ignore them. Having a nurse and cook, which
they could afford, freed her and my dad to be with us. We
had dinner with our parents. We played charades and
twenty questions, hung out in the den together, watching
the news, *College Bowl* (a quiz show), Sid Caesar and
Imogene Coca in *Your Show of Shows* (which was the
1950s *Saturday Night Live*). We sang rounds. This was
family life "before" and, remarkably, even part of family
life "after."

With me, she was never cozy or intimate. I never remember her hugging or kissing me. Nevertheless, her
presence was powerful. In all the ideas she had for our

lives. In the example of her life (the good version). In the structure—down to eggs and bacon for breakfast on Monday, Tuesday, Thursday, and Friday. Pancakes on Wednesday, Saturday I forget, Sunday deli. No cereal. She was certain bran was bad for us. She never said or confided; she distilled and proclaimed. I lived my life by the Book of Mom.

One of her rules—"Your homework is your problem. I will never get involved"—had an exception: "But I will write your graduation speech." And she did. She sat down and banged out my eighth grade graduation speech on her typewriter. Naturally I got chosen and delivered her speech. The theme was "Beyond the Blue Horizon," and the last line was, "I will look beyond the blue horizon for a better and more peaceful world." Which, for my mother, has an irony so obvious it hurts to point it out.

It mattered so much to her that I shine at graduation—vanity, probably, since it was one of the few events she attended and her daughters were part of her myth—she couldn't entrust writing the speech to me (wisely, I think).

I was proud of her, too. Which is another reason it's hard to write about her. "Never tell anyone what happens here." It's a plea: *Don't diminish me.*

So the daytime version of her: the most accomplished

woman in the room with a pride of daughters. She never even lost her temper. Nights she went to pieces, unable to process pain or anger except to spew it. She was unintegrated. Superego or id. Take your pick. Being that—think about it—how terrifying. What a phenomenal disconnect. My poor mother. I'm sure she terrified herself. She was disassembling nightly. She was human global warming—norms replaced by extremes.

My mother's drinking was so overwhelming that I didn't notice the obvious: that my dad was drinking, too. This staggering myopia resulted in the lifelong belief (I'm sure shared with other children of alcoholics) that, when I am looking left, something is coming at me from the right. I am always trying to look in two directions at once, which is impossible.

When everything went topsy-turvy, I constructed a narrative, a way to make sense of it, to understand. My mother was responsible. She was the guilty party. I simplified everything—the complications were beyond me. She was the aggressor: she got drunk, left her room, the fights began. She was genuinely scary—a shapeshifter—and my dad wasn't.

Also, my dad was nice to me, interested in me, appreciative. (I usually think of my mother as my mother and my father as my dad, and that tells you a lot.) I confided in him when I was upset about school or friends, and he sympathized. We hung out. I went to the grocery store with him to shop and to the deli on Sunday. We played tennis, he took me to tennis matches, I watched football with him. I was a tomboy and loved to play football. He always bragged that if I were a boy, I'd be a great end (not the block and tackle kind, the one that runs for passes). I became his confidante, his ally in their epic battles. I hoped he would leave her and I could live with him. I am sure, looking back, that I thought he loved me more than he loved her, which he did not. I was completely wrong about that. Love can be monstrous. Theirs was. They were George and Martha in *Who's Afraid of Virginia Woolf?* Seeing that play was like hanging out with my parents in our living room at three a.m. My parents were proof of what a sick, screwed-up, perfect thing marriage can be.

How could I ever understand that? I was a kid.

Children of alcoholics are always in over their heads.

Thank God for my sister Amy. Amy was my partner, emotionally, and in the futile attempt to stop my mother from drinking. And them from fighting. Together we would sneak down the stairs and dilute the liquor bottles.

As if we had the power to stop them. How sweet. How in-nocent. That we thought there was something we could do to stop alcoholics full of rage, thirsting for battle.

Which is another reason it's hard to write about my mother. I can't separate her from my dad. Not this part. Not the sick part. My parents were fused.

Once my mother kicked me out. I was on his side, she said, which was true. "Go away and never ever, ever come back." That sounds like a line from a children's book. Maybe it is. I have blocked out exactly what she said. Maurice Sendak, whose work I love, understood the scary world of childhood. If your parents are drunks, however, there is no waking up in bed the way Max does in *Where the Wild Things Are.* There is no realizing you are safe after all.

This happened during the day. I was about sixteen, and by this time the nights had begun to bleed into the days (Hyde was taking over—Hyde was the bad one, in case, like me, you get him and Jekyll mixed up). When she kicked me out, I walked to my friend Stephanie's, which took about a half hour. Stephanie lived with her mom and brother (her father had died) in an apartment south of Olympic. In Beverly Hills, this was considered the other side of the tracks. Stephanie had a really nice mom. I was crazy about her mom. The difference in our families was a classic lesson in how money can't buy happiness. After two days at Stephanie's, I went home. My mother said nothing, neither did my dad. Alcoholics don't have a lot of follow-through.

I can't help notice that, in writing about my mother, I keep sliding into me. Into what she did to me. What I'm writing—my intention to get a grip on her—keeps spinning out of control, the way life in that house did. I keep trying to make this essay "neat," bend it to my will, make it track, but I can't. And I keep waking up at two in the morning with my mother on my mind.

Sleeping through the night—because I rarely did after age eleven—is one of my favorite things. Once I moved out, I became a champion sleeper. Now my mother's back, jolting me awake, rattling my brain.

This awareness is hyperfocus at work. Here I am writing about my mom at the same time trying to analyze what's going on while I am writing about my mom. My brain is in overdrive, over-thinking. This analyzing upon analyzing puts layers of distance between myself and her. Which is how I like it. Although it's not surprising that in writing about my mother, I'm writing about me. Because: Who is the mother here? Not my mother. Not if Amy and I are trying to keep her safe by diluting bottles of Scotch.

She was chic, stylish. Wore suits with a gold bow pin on her lapel—the bow studded with tiny rubies had a large rectangular topaz dangling from it. Her jewelry, like her style, never varied. I have the pin. It looks terrible on me because it's big, but it's absolutely her. She always looked smart, with her wavy hair brushed back off her face, little or no makeup.

She loved to give parties. Any event meant a party. Election night, the Academy Awards, the Rose Bowl. I remember so fondly the scrambled eggs she made for forty people at halftime. My mother thought you should cook eggs slowly. I have a feeling Nora's written about her eggs, but don't have the patience to look it up. Congress could have passed the budget in the time it took my mom to scramble eggs. They were delicious and pretty, a very buttery yellow—she used almost more butter than eggs. Thanks to her, I believe the best kind of party to throw is one where everyone comes over and watches television. I've thrown parties to watch ice skating championships.

All this went on while my mother descended further and further into madness. My parents wrote several more funny, light, charming movies, including the adaptations of *Carousel* and *Desk Set* with Tracy and Hepburn. They collaborated on a Broadway play, *Take Her, She's Mine*, based on Nora's leaving for college, ostensibly about our family but in fact having absolutely nothing to do with what went on at home. My mother wrote a play of her own. It was extraordinary that she kept going given how messed up she was—extraordinary that she kept working and that they kept collaborating given their hellish relationship.

Eventually, however, they did stop, because times changed, what they wrote wasn't relevant or wanted, and because alcohol took over.

I bumped into my mother on the street once when I was in my early twenties. I was walking with a friend on New York City's Upper East Side, which is where my parents eventually decamped, and there she was. We chatted a minute about absolutely nothing in particular, and my friend and I walked on. I don't remember who I was with and I don't remember what my mother and I said to each other except that it was so impersonal that my friend was stunned by it. If I hadn't said, "Hi, Mom," my friend would never have known we were related.

The day version of her was a great gift—a sense of destiny, identity, structure, discipline, drive. As a woman she was far ahead of the curve. To the night version of her I owe free-floating anxiety. I am no longer a child in an unsafe home, but anxiety became habit. My brain is conditioned. I worry. I recheck everything obsessively. Is the seat belt fastened, are the reservations correct, is my passport in my purse? Have I done something wrong? Have I said something wrong? I'm sorry—whatever happened must be my fault. Is everyone all right, and if they aren't, how can I step in? That brilliant serenity prayer: God give me the serenity to accept the things I cannot change. To all children of alcoholics I want to say, Good luck with that. If I don't do it myself, it won't get done (this belief is often rewarded in this increasingly incompetent world). Also, I panic easily. I am not the person you want sitting in the exit row of an airplane. And distrust. Just in general, distrust. Irony.

Irony, according to the dictionary, is the use of comedy to distance oneself from emotion. I developed it as a child lickety-split. Irony was armor, a way to stick it to Mom. You think you can get me? Come on, shoot me, aim that arrow straight at my heart. It can't make a dent because I'm wearing irony.

But she did get to me. My most powerful memory is of going downstairs in the middle of the night to where they were battling, throwing myself on the floor (I was a teenager), and screaming, flipping out. And my mother said, cool as can be, "Get up, you're faking." So I did. I stopped and got up.

For many years, I thought she was right: I had been faking. But I don't think so.

. . . .

When my mother was dying, my friend Susan went to visit her in the hospital. Susan was my college roommate, and we shared an apartment for several years after graduating. I had no idea Susan visited my mom. She confessed it only recently.

Susan had often accompanied me when I went to see my parents. For protection. Well, more for moral support. My mother was mean to Susan, too, chiding her (although Susan was brilliant and found it, she claims, ridiculous) that she wasn't so smart and couldn't even do a crossword puzzle, which my mother was great at—that and the *New York Times* acrostic. Susan went to visit her in the hospital, and my mother said to Susan, "Bring me a bottle of Chivas."

Susan did, figuring what did it matter anyway.

So, last words:

"Take notes."

"I hated crocheting."

"Bring me a bottle of Chivas."

How did it come to that? How did it, for that incredibly accomplished woman, all come down to wanting one more drink?

What I know: My father cheated. I didn't know it then. When I was a kid and the fights were raging, I thought—gleaning from what I overheard—that my dad had kissed another woman at a party. In retrospect, this seems woefully naive, but truly it was one of the few facts I could pluck from the chaos. Facts were not easy to come by at our house. As I remember, although I am not sure about this, I viewed this betrayal as minor, more a curiosity than a cause. It only confused me: How could that cause this? As I said, I was a daddy's girl. Still their fights, as I heard them/recall them, didn't have narrative. A coherent plotline. Logic. This accusation surfaced only now and then. Reality was obfuscated. There was no apparent evidence that my dad was out gallivanting. My parents were always together. When my dad wasn't with my mom, he was with us. That's the way it seemed.

Then, long after she died, he wrote a garbled confessional memoir that he gave to my husband with the admonition not to show it to me. I read it anyway. A depressingly familiar Hollywood story—a weak man let loose in a candy store. Success and a modicum of fame and glamour screws up a lot of people. Am I letting him off the hook even now? I don't know.

And I don't know how much my mother knew. Still, when she said "I hated crocheting," was she settling a score, my misplaced loyalty to my dad, or was she simply scattershot mean, or did she just not really like me?

Did she just not really like me? I wrote that so easily, and yet, more to the point: Did she not like me when she was drunk, but like me when she was sober? Who was she really? The night mom or the day mom? Will the real mom please stand up?

My dad's memoir was not the story of a man who had character, that's for sure. Or any self-awareness. Do I think it was true? In the overall. His other book, *We Thought We Could Do Anything*, however, was a well of misinformation, including the year I was born. Over time I heard him change his Hollywood stories, the ones he loved to tell about stars he knew or what happened on the set. As a result I never believe anyone's Hollywood story, because the point of it, at least for my dad, was not the story, but being able to tell it: *I know this, I was there.*

Does my father's cheating explain my mother's self-destruction? Not to me. President Clinton humiliated Hillary time and time again. She became a senator and then secretary of state. Her husband cheated and she traveled to 109 countries negotiating things like treaties. My mother's beloved brother died when I was eight or nine or so, I'm not sure exactly. Did that contribute to her alcoholic collapse? Maybe. Maybe not. Cause and effect? There is no inevitable. Nothing neat and simple. My mother had a whopping genetic predisposition to alcohol and demons I can't begin to guess at.

Which is why I can't write about my mother. I have no idea who she was.

COLLABORATION

"Forgive me if I tend to romanticize the past." That's the beginning—nearly the beginning—of the Woody Allen memory movie about childhood, *Radio Days*, perhaps my favorite movie ever. "Forgive me if I tend to romanticize the past" is his voice over a sepia-drenched, windy, rainy Far Rockaway. That's how I remember my first collaboration with Nora: bathed in nostalgia.

Before I discuss collaboration, however, a bit about screenwriting.

There comes a point in every screenwriter's life when she or he has to decide: Do I want to be a director or do I want to be angry?

There are many things to say about being a screenwriter,

much of it positive, but this is the most important: Screen-writers get fired. You are hired and you are fired. Often, when you are fired, if your script isn't going to die on a shelf, another screenwriter replaces you.

Even when you are not fired, when you have man-aged to survive the often byzantine development process, once the script is on its way to production, you are kissed good-bye. And that's sad, because that is when the fun begins. When everyone gets to make a movie. Because of your script, hundreds of people may get to work in all sorts of creative and interesting ways. Because of your script, if you shoot on a location, a whole town gets a boost economically and has an adventure. The screenwriter, however, doesn't have a job on a set. Everyone else is col-laborating now, contributing their particular expertise, but your work is essentially done. You could be bored wit-less. Nevertheless, it's nice to be welcome, nice when the director welcomes you. Maybe three minutes out of the day you will notice something, or get asked a question, or realize your intent is being compromised by the way the scene is being shot, or something might be funnier an-other way—some random three minutes in a twelve-hour day—and you better hope you are paying attention. You might instead be at craft services (where the food is) wolf-ing down a sandwich. Craft services on Nora's movies were always spectacular, no surprise. Parties and movies were a bit mixed up in her head, at least in the beginning. Which reminds me that before we shot *Sleepless in Seattle* we all had a cherry pie tasting.

Nothing is more seductive than screenwriting. It is playful. Not easy, but so much fun it has the illusion of easy. There are books on screenwriting, so I won't ramble on about how to do it (and Nora has written about it, too, so forgive any repetition here), but every time you write a screenplay, you are seduced. You fall in love. You think you are safe. *They will make this for sure. This script will never get lost in development hell. You will never be replaced. Not on this one. This is good.*

But no writer is safe. And since I'm complaining about the good life, forgive me, I'm going to keep on for a short time. "Notes" are criticisms and requests for changes that a screenwriter gets from everyone, especially from all the collaborators who are your bosses, higher-ups on the food chain—studio executives, producers, occasionally producers' children, actors (almost always good ones from actors). I've never received notes from a book editor the way I do from a studio executive. In my experience, a book editor is trying to help you get where you need to go. With a movie, what they want may have nothing to do with what you want or what they told you they wanted to begin with, which they didn't realize was all wrong until they read your script. A book editor gives compliments. Studio executives and many producers should go to compliment school. They barely spend a second on what's good before they're off to what they want changed. And this is, excuse the expression, stupid. Because knowing what's working is as important as knowing what isn't. Where's the gold? Tell me. Then I can mine it further. Writers write better if they're appreciated. Everyone does better work if they're appreciated. Elementary, my dear Watson. Screenwriters often compliment the person giving them notes. What a good note, they say. They do this because they have low self-esteem, which they acquired from being screenwriters. Screenwriters might also think brownnosing makes them safer, less likely to be fired. It does not.

A director comes on and either wants to write it himself/herself or has a writer they love to work with, or the actor has a writer he or she never leaves home without, or the studio wants it funnier, or the studio decides they want another "take," another "tone." Really, half the time you have no idea why you've been fired because there is a lot of lying. If it's not lying, it's spinning. You can be spun so fast or cleverly, you don't even know which direction you are facing. With some producers it's practically an art form. Even producers who are friends, who are helpful and smart, whom you like and respect and who like and respect you, will ax you if a studio/director/actor wants it. It's not surprising the business of screenwriting happens in Los Angeles, the land of earthquakes, because the ground is never solid under you.

Nora and I once did an adaptation of a charming book, *Flipped* by Wendelin Van Draanen. Rob Reiner came on to direct. The same Rob Reiner who had directed *When Harry Met Sally*. So Nora had history with him, good history. A relationship. He dumped us and wrote a script of his own. (And asked us to cut our bonus, but never mind.) We had nothing to do with his movie.

Inevitably many screenwriters feel insulted, jilted, or powerless. And it's confusing—how can they be miserable if they are so lucky to be screenwriters? Half the world wants to be a screenwriter. How *can* they be miserable? They have no right, they are spoiled.

Even if they are successful and have a movie well made, even beautifully made, eventually screenwriters still want it their way. They want the movie the way they imagined it. If something they wrote isn't captured properly cinematically, they would prefer it to be their own fault. This can only happen if a screenwriter directs his own script. I'm generalizing here, but not wildly.

Nora had reached that time when she had to choose— anger or direct. She chose direct. You have to be awfully successful to make that choice. She was and she did. She had a wonderful book, *This Is Your Life* by Meg Wolitzer, about two sisters (Erica, sixteen, and Opal, ten) and their single mom (Dottie), who decides to follow her dream of becoming a stand-up comic. Nora asked if I would write it with her. She didn't want, she said, to set off on this voyage alone. She needed help, someone she trusted. She needed a collaborator. The material was perfect for us.

At the time Nora was living in New York and I was in Los Angeles, remarried happily, with two stepchildren. I had worked as a journalist at *New York* magazine and had had several books published, books of humor and essays. I had just begun my screenwriting career—my husband, a screenwriter, taught me how to do it—and I had completed two commissioned but unmade scripts, one based on my book *Teenage Romance*. Nora had just had her tremendous success with *When Harry Met Sally*.

This collaboration was fantastic for me. I wasn't going to get fired. No way would my sister fire me, and she was the director. It was a great adventure creatively. A leap. An adventure in sisterhood, too. As Nora had promised, the material was perfect, all common ground: sisters, a working mother, female dilemmas, the stuff of female relationships that American movies are rarely about, and show business, which we grew up around.

Our goal with *This Is My Life* was to launch her directing career. That might seem obvious, but what I mean is the movie didn't have to be a big hit (although of course we had dreams), but it had to be good enough to land her a second. That's another reason we were happy that the material was nearly autobiographical. It gave Nora a comfort zone. It raised the odds of her directing a movie that worked.

Most of my writing up to that time had been about children, which I knew meant I was bringing something Nora needed to the writing mix. We began traveling back and forth between Los Angeles and New York, doing the hard work of finding the movie in the book, then outlining, writing scenes, exchanging scenes. That time is mostly a blur of hanging out in my office or hers, sometimes in her kitchen at her round table, taking breaks for eating and shopping. It was before our wearing-only-black phase (at least it was before mine because I was living in LA, which I think of as baby-blue land). There was a lot more to buy.

Neither of us quite knew what we were doing. I was learning more and more about screenwriting, and she had never directed. Both being somewhat ignorant, we needed each other for skill as well as emotional support. Also, it was fun (not to mention easier) to collaborate. Nora and I would say to each other, I almost got this, please finish it, or we need a joke here, or why isn't this working?—send the scene off and back it came, done.

The movie, renamed *This Is My Life*, starred Julie Kavner, Samantha Mathis, and Gaby Hoffmann, with supporting roles played by Dan Aykroyd and Carrie Fisher (and an original score by Carly Simon). Because it was low-budget, there was an in-the-trenches feel to the shoot. We all stayed in the same Toronto hotel, hung out nights in the bar, and we laughed. We laughed all the time.

We also drank tons of water. I remember this very clearly, and oddly it's barely all I remember specifically— the set of *This Is My Life* was the first time I noticed everyone walking around with plastic bottles of Evian and taking sips. I started doing it, too. Every woman who works in the movie business has a bottle of water in her purse. Hydration is a big deal.

. . . .

Collaboration, I discovered, is a kind of marriage. Like marriage, it works best when you both want the same things, like the same things, and laugh at the same things. Shared sensibility is critical. Loyalty, too. And trust. You should also be a little bit in love with each other's brains.

Since collaboration is a kind of marriage, it follows, theoretically speaking, that if the collaborators are already related, it's incest. Incest because, well, you are making babies. I always think of my books and movies as babies. Although now that I have had that sick thought, I will try to banish it. Let's just say collaboration between relatives is a kind of incest. This might account for the twisted weirdness of the Coen brothers' movies, although probably, like Nora and me, Joel and Ethan Coen share half a brain. This freaky/creepy posit should be a warning to Judd Apatow, who is now collaborating with his entire nuclear family.

The other day I was discussing collaboration with my screenwriter friend Alex. He collaborates with another friend, Brian. Their wives have become close friends. Alex feels, he said, as if he's living in a Mormon marriage.

I saw a new print of *This Is My Life* recently (I hadn't watched the movie in years). It was screened at MoMA. I heard Nora's and my voices so clearly—me more in the sisters, her more in the mother, but really it was harmony. Deeply personal for both of us. It's my belief, in terms of collaboration, deeply personal is rare.

Rare . . . partly, I think—excuse this theoretical diversion—because collaboration dilutes intimacy. The intimacy you have with your own thoughts, your passions and quirks that you can access if you work alone, in isolation. Thoughts you might feel freer to access if you didn't need to please the other person. This requirement to please inevitably means that there is, in every collaboration, the potential for conflict. But I did not know this when Nora and I started writing together.

This Is My Life opened at the Sundance Film Festival and was released in New York, Chicago, and LA. The studio was going to release it wide (across the country) if its grosses were high enough, but they weren't. Whether the world will love your movie as much as you do is always a question, but at least your collaborator will. And that is a comfort. Nevertheless, it did the trick. Just as we'd hoped, Nora got offered a second chance: *Sleepless in Seattle.*

Our collaboration was a fortress—us against the unpredictable, whimsical movie business, where there is jealousy and competitiveness and tough times in addition to great and glamorous ones. The movie business knows how to insult you better than it knows anything. Where you park, where you sit, where your table is located, when your call is returned, if your call is returned. On the Warner lot is an original 1928 building where the executive offices are located. In front of the building is a circular driveway. Small. Room for very few cars. We knew *You've Got Mail* was going to be made not only because Tom Hanks had agreed to star . . . or because, as our producer Lauren Shuler Donner told us, the copresident of Warner, Bill Gerber, believed in it . . . but because of the driveway. That's where we got to park.

. . . .

Temperamentally, Nora was more suited to the movie business than I am. She was tough and could intimidate. Knew how to intimidate. No one understood the power of silence better than she did. Just not saying anything. She understood fame. Even before she was famous, she had an East Coast cachet. Then she became famous herself— and fame is worshipped in the movie business because it's what everyone is after. Fame is power. Studios love doing business with stars. If a star could do everything there is to do on a movie, studio executives would be happier. They might protest, but in fact it would make them giddy all the time. Stars make everyone giddy. This is one reason actors always win Oscars in non-actor categories, for instance when they direct or write (Emma Thompson, Matt Damon, Ben Affleck, Mel Gibson and Clint Eastwood, to name a few). Of course, that also happens because actors are the largest wing of Academy voters, and they like to vote for themselves. I'm generalizing here, but not wildly.

Working with Nora in Hollywood was like traveling in an armored vehicle. Once she left a studio meeting for a few minutes and everyone fell on me, giving me all the script notes they didn't have the nerve to tell her. This happened as well on our movie sets all the time. And I, blessed (or doomed) to be the middle child—always understanding everyone else's point of view—would tell Nora their notes/concerns/complaints, which she sometimes listened to and as frequently dismissed with a face. From seeing it so often, I can make the face, too. It's just scrunching up a bit, nothing too extreme.

While I was often an intermediary, I wasn't a pushover. I want to say that right here and now. I never recommended anything I didn't agree with.

What prepared me best for this role, however—lobbying Nora for changes (ones I wanted and ones others did that I agreed with)—was not being a middle child. It was being a stepmother. A stepmother has no direct control over her stepkids. Not really. She has to convince the more "legitimate" parent that her opinion/idea is right. With our baby the movie, Nora the director was the more legitimate parent. So what I was doing at home with my husband, Jerry, lobbying him endlessly about his kids, I was also doing on the set.

I often drove her crazy because I was certain she wasn't going to do what I wanted even when she promised she would. I would tell her the same thing twelve times. I was right, she didn't always listen. Sometimes she would boss me around, and then I would go home and try to boss my husband around. This did not go over well. As my friend Alex said, a Mormon marriage.

. . . .

Each movie Nora and I did had its own anatomy. The first was the purest, just us. *Sleepless in Seattle*, on the other hand, was based on a script by Jeff Arch, rewritten by David Ward, then by Nora, and then by both of us. Even though we didn't collaborate directly with those writers, we built on their scripts. Tom Hanks had a lot of input, too. On his character. He was very demanding—we had to repeatedly juice up his scenes—and I learned from him about writing for stars: how stars need stuff, interesting stuff, how they have to drive the action.

What I remember most about the *Sleepless* shoot, however, was the car accident I had on the day I arrived. In an underground parking garage with those giant cement columns every few feet, I backed into a man's brand-new Lexus. It still had dealer plates. The car didn't have a scratch on it, but the driver went ballistic. He kept shouting that maybe it had internal injuries. And I kept saying, "It's not a person." But this is the amazing part, the part about moviemaking I can never get over: All I had to do was call someone in the production office, tell them I smashed my fender (mine was a bit dented), they picked me up, and the next day I had a new rental car. I never had to think about it again. What I'm saying is, working on a movie can spoil a girl rotten.

On *Michael* we rewrote a script by Pete Dexter, the novelist, and Jim Quinlan, a journalist who had worked in the tabloids (the world the story takes place in). Here's the nasty on being a screenwriter: After being replaced yourself, after having your heart broken or sort of, you go and replace someone else. In fact, you are thrilled to do it. A rewrite. Good money. We did this on *Sleepless* and *Michael*, believing the screenplay needed us to fix it and wanting it to be Nora's/ours. In other words, every screenwriter, whether or not she or he has a collaborator, is a collaborator—not in the good sense of the word. More like Vichy and the Germans in World War II. They collaborate with a system that mistreats them. Screenwriters are pitted against one another—the weak against the weak.

Dexter and Quinlan invented the grubby, irresistible archangel that John Travolta brought to life. The character of Michael was their creation. I don't think anyone except Travolta could have played that part. It was our great good fortune that he did. The script had been in turnaround (this is when a studio doesn't want to make it and gives you some time to place it at another studio). In this case, the studio releasing the movie, in an attempt to make it hard for us to cast it, gave us a list of actors that we couldn't use. Studios are always worried they are going to put something in turnaround that will turn out to be *E.T.*, a humongous turnaround embarrassment. How do you explain to the world and the stockholders such a creative and, more important to them, economic miscalculation? Universal gave us a no-Michael list, but Travolta wasn't on it.

Mixed Nuts, based on the French comedy *Le père Noël est une ordure* (translation: *Santa Claus Is a Shit*), was a flop. Starring Steve Martin, it was about six misfits at a suicide hotline center on Christmas Eve. In retrospect, a flop is obvious. Of course. What were we thinking? Many of life's flops, like marriages, are obvious in retrospect. If you knew it, you wouldn't do it, but you didn't, so you did. Probably Nora and I should never have tried to adapt something French. We are so not French. French comedies are French in the most peculiarly French way, largely because they're played by French people.

I loved the shoot, however. In the magical land of moviemaking, artists of all sorts collaborate. Being on a set and/or being involved with the entire moviemaking process, not simply writing (and I was fortunate to be welcome), means you learn from everyone—from your producer, casting person (casting sessions teach a writer whether their scene works or how it might work better), editor (film editors are temperamentally the most like writers and, in my experience, very generous with their knowledge), costume, makeup, production designer. You see them work, they share, and you absorb. On *Mixed Nuts*, I got to know Sven Nykvist, the brilliant cinematographer who had shot many of Ingmar Bergman's films. He had shot *Sleepless* as well, but on *Mixed Nuts*, I hung out with him on night shoots, of which there were many—balmy LA nights under the palm trees near Venice Beach. He would tell me how and why he would frame and light the shots. He could light a shot with candles and was famous for doing it in a Bergman masterpiece called *Fanny and Alexander*. I treasure those memories. I have a photo in my office of Sven and me talking, sitting on the set in director's chairs—him, a hulking Swedish guy with a Swedish beard (a hedgelike trim around his chin that never looks good on any man, but looked great on Sven), wearing a wide-brimmed white straw hat with a black band. My face is mostly obscured by a baseball cap, the ubiquitous movie-set headgear.

Sven, seventy-two then, was a movie animal (my term)—someone who was alive only on a set. Everything else that movie animals do is what you might call "between." He had worked on sets since he was seventeen, he told me. He had houses in Europe he rarely visited. I think he had wives, too, he never saw when he had them, although he didn't have one then. He had groupies who hung about, mostly at the hotel. Until I met Sven, I didn't know cinematographers had groupies. The night we wrapped, he flew to Sweden (perhaps it was Norway) to start another film, *Kristin Lavransdatter.* Liv Ullmann was directing this movie, based on an epic novel (think Swedish *Gone with the Wind*). It takes place in the Middle Ages. I had read the book in college. Every time a man leaves the house, he is eaten by a bear. Every time a woman has sex, she gets pregnant. Bear/pregnant. Bear/pregnant.

Sven died ten years later, after shooting four more features and a few documentaries. He had been the cinematographer on more than 108 movies, according to his IMDb page. Thanks to the wonderful world of movie collaboration, I got to spend time with him.

. . . .

Here's a weird thing about collaborating with a sister: Some people you work with can't be friends with both of you. "Friends" doesn't quite describe it, because Nora and I didn't often share friends. They can't relate to both sisters. I don't know why, and I don't know whether it's true when the collaborators are brothers. People feel they have to choose. They simply can't like both of you. Not always, but it happened often enough that I wondered about it. I wondered if they were bringing their own sibling problems into the mix.

Having said that, one of the remarkable things about moviemaking is how many collaborators become life-long friends. The closest thing to a location shoot is camp (at least our shoots, because they were friendly; some don't have that atmosphere). You're all away from your real lives in a strange place, which breeds an intensity and an intimacy. It's as if you'd all gotten lost in the woods together, fallen out of a canoe, hiked miles, and killed a snake. To survive, you had to trust one another.

You've Got Mail was an especially good collaboration because, once again, we had tons of common ground. We set it in the world of books. We both loved books, had grown up in a house where books were worshipped. In 1996, which this was, big chain stores were putting independent booksellers out of business, which was not only personally upsetting but gave us a perfect plot for the most important romantic comedy element: Why can't two people be together? In this case, he was putting her out of business. (How quickly things change—now Amazon is destroying the chains and the independents are staging a comeback.) We both loved children's books. That's why Meg Ryan/Kathleen Kelly has a children's bookstore. We set the movie on the Upper West Side of New York City, where we were both then living, in the same building as a matter of fact. To collaborate, we had only to cross a courtyard. Also we were both crazy about *The Shop Around the Corner*, the 1940 movie on which *You've Got Mail* is based.

Actually the movie began life in 1937 as a Hungarian play, *Parfumerie*, by Miklós László. Then came *The Shop Around the Corner*, followed by a musical version, *In the Good Old Summertime* (1949), followed by *She Loves Me*, a Broadway musical (1963). The score by Sheldon Harnick and Jerry Bock is divine.

This is rare—when a story and characters are so winning that they continue to inspire and enchant. The plot is simple: A man and a woman, pen pals (in our update, e-mail-pals), are in love in their letters but hate each other in person. They have no idea they know each other . . . and then one of them finds out. In writing *You've Got Mail*, we collaborated not only with each other but in spirit with Samson Raphaelson, who wrote both previous movies, and with the original playwright as well. It was an honor.

. . . .

Sometime during our third movie, which was *Mixed Nuts*, I started writing novels. I didn't want to be a director and I didn't want to be angry. Fortunately I had another path. Faith Sale, an editor at Putnam, offered me a contract. Books were my first love. I needed to tell stories my way. I needed to hear my own voice. My idea of an ideal workday is six hours alone in a room. That means, by temperament, I'm not a director, and truly a movie belongs to the director. That's the dilemma of screenwriting. A movie isn't writing. It's based on writing. The movie wouldn't exist without a script, but it isn't a script. Screenwriters have to live with that truth. A lot of time they live in denial. A movie is a visual medium. Bottom line: If you don't *see* something in a movie, odds are, you don't remember it.

My favorite movie memories are often random moments seen, not spoken. In *Radio Days*, a complex back-and-forth between Woody Allen's fictionalized 1940s childhood and the glamorous life of the folks on the radio, in this film dense with character and funny lines, what pops to mind: Mr. Zipsky. Is it even a minute? I don't think so. Mr. Zipsky in his boxer shorts, waving a meat cleaver, runs amok down the street to the tune of "Mairzy Doats." I love that.

I had not gotten a credit on *Sleepless.* Three other writers did. That fact did not push me into novels—the luck of receiving the offer did—but no question it made me aware that I needed to do it. The Writers Guild decides who gets credit when more than one writer is involved. In Jeff Arch's original, the leading man/Tom Hanks goes on the radio himself to say he needs a new wife. David Ward made a critical story/structural change: His son called the radio. Nora had done a draft, and then when she was hired to direct, I came on to do the final draft. All the other writers had made major structural changes. I hadn't, and to the Writers Guild that is big stuff, rightfully so. Nora called to tell me. I remember where I was sitting, at my husband's desk. Even though we expected it and I laughed, I remember it, so it wasn't nothing. Ever generous (and a bit guilty), Nora gave me a cut of profit points and an associate producer credit. The movie did go into profit, although the studio had to be sued to admit it.

At this moment, I'm suddenly thinking about something Nora said that has nothing to do with the movies. Shortly before she entered the hospital, she had a conversation with our dentist about a temporary inlay she had.

She said to Dr. Bruno, "I can't discuss this now. I have low platelets and I'm going to lunch at Grenouille." (La Grenouille is an elegant old-world New York restaurant.) This line, as much irony as pluck and so adorable, sums up how much fun mattered to Nora. It was always part of the equation. In our collaboration, her energy was contagious, unflagging, and always buoyed me—even on set, when we were exhausted or the shoot was difficult. (One cannot overstate the potential for hysteria on a movie set. Everyone always acts as if making the movie is as important as eradicating malaria.) But this funny/sad/dear thing she said also popped to mind because of La Grenouille, because I'm thinking about how absolutely impossible Nora was when it came to choosing a restaurant. She would say, Where should we eat? and eventually we would decide to eat where she wanted to eat, which she definitely knew before she asked the question. She needed decisions to be hers . . . not only where we would eat, but what we would work on. She was not simply a director of movies, she was the director of life. And she was my older sister, too. *Quel* nightmare. This was another reason why I wanted to write novels. I wanted control, too. I needed to fly solo.

As we both got more confident and needed each other less, we began to drive each other more nuts. Once I sat down to write a scene and typed two letters—that's letters, not words—and she said, "No." I swear this is true, not that you'd doubt it if you knew her. I banished her immediately: "Go make lunch." She made us the best lunches. I'm always remembering her standing at the kitchen counter with her perfect hair, flats, long shirt, and skinny pants, tossing mesclun salad in a bowl. And by the way, I snapped at her often, although how is this possible, nothing comes to mind. Sibling relationships are essentially primitive. Nora bit into a tomato when she was seven or so in such a perfect way as to spray juice in my eye. That is my first memory of us. I don't remember torturing Hallie, although I'm sure Hallie remembers. I told Amy that a little blue man lived under her bed and would get her in the middle of the night. Sisters share an uncivilized history. Now and then, as adults and as collaborators, it surfaced.

Sibling stuff got in the way on *Hanging Up*. *Hanging Up* was my novel. I remember Nora phoning—she read it on her way to Los Angeles and called as soon as the plane landed to say she loved it and we should do it as a movie. This meant we would adapt the book together and she would direct, and we would do it at Sony with Larry Mark (whom we both loved) producing. I was thrilled.

Another studio was interested, which meant a different creative team, but for me there was no contest. *Hanging Up*, based on my relationship with my dad, was the story of three sisters coming to terms with the death of a difficult father. The heroine was, like me, a middle child. The minute we began, we were crankier than usual. We had never adapted anything that belonged to one of us originally.

Hanging Up, I discovered, was too personal to me for a writing collaboration. Our father had died when Nora was shooting a movie (*Sleepless*). Nora was away, Hallie in Boston. The responsibility and burden had been primarily Amy's and mine. That history played out when we began writing. I was edgy, harboring resentment, and she was territorial as always, but also she needed this to be her story—it was her father, too. Whose dad was it, whose story, whose way? At some point after completing the first draft, we disagreed about the script so much that we stopped speaking for at least a month—or at most we spoke when necessary. This was the only time in our lives that such a thing happened. We were both miserable.

We ended up deciding, for the sake of our sisterhood, that we needed another director. Diane Keaton came on.

Today, missing Nora as much as I do, I find it sad that

we couldn't negotiate our way through this so she could direct, and yet I still find it inevitable that we ended up in a struggle.

All longtime collaborations eventually or occasionally get thorny. That's my guess. Given ego, talent, investment, life—at some point you and your writing companion are not going to be on the same page.

Because Nora began shooting *You've Got Mail*, I wrote the final draft of *Hanging Up*. Diane Keaton gave great script notes, which helped in doing a draft that everyone loved and having Meg Ryan commit (a dream come true), but the movie itself, the final result, doesn't feel as if it belongs to me or Nora. I didn't recognize the tone. It was much broader than our script. Tone is such a powerful element. And visually the world of the movie wasn't what I imagined, either. To complicate things, the shoot was compromised—Walter Matthau got sick and couldn't complete the movie as written. It had to be edited to accommodate the fact that he was missing. Keaton didn't enjoy collaboration the way Nora and I did. Like many directors, once she was in preproduction—from then on through shooting and the editing process—she didn't consult the writer.

Because Keaton was the director, the movie became

hers. It made me very happy that I had written *Hanging Up* as a novel. It also exists my way.

Flash forward.

Love, Loss, and What I Wore, Nora's and my last baby, was based on the small, powerful, illustrated memoir by Ilene Beckerman. It was the story of her life told through the clothes she wore, and the awesome thing about the book was that even though it was completely specific (about her life and her clothes), reading it opened a floodgate of memories about what-you-wore-when.

Nora found the book and fell in love with it. And she knew it was a play, a *Vagina Monologues* sort of thing. And I am eternally grateful, because it was pure joy. Eventually.

We always called it *The Vagina Monologues* without the vaginas, but then we got a message from *The Vagina Monologues* people that we should stop, although, hello, free speech, we kept on. And could not fathom why they didn't consider it a compliment.

We optioned the book in 1996, and the play opened Off-Broadway in 2009. Fourteen years later. The world's longest birth.

The play was based on this simple idea: If you ask women about their clothes, they tell you about their lives.

To make this history short, because it wasn't, we knew that Ilene Beckerman (Gingy, as she is called) would be only one story in the play. The rest would be ours and our friends'. We sent out e-mails to all our girlfriends—tell us about your clothes. And they did. We shaped their stories, adapted, or, in some cases, did very little. We separately interviewed to find other dramas we needed and added our own. Then we had a weeklong workshop. That's when you develop the play with actors—gathering in a rehearsal space (in this case a room like a dance studio) to explore the material and characters, rewrite, and on the last day invite friends and possibly backers to attend a read-through. A read-through should tell you if the play works—if it's funny, moving, cohesive, dramatic. Our play was only occasionally those things, and our friends were not impressed.

Nora and I continued to work on it sporadically and had another workshop and reading—I'm not certain of the time, but a year later at least. Again a disappointment. Especially the character of Gingy. We couldn't nail her. She was charming and inviting in the book (and in person as a matter of fact), but not in our play, not onstage.

We gave up and let the option lapse.

Several years later, Nora phoned and said she was doing another workshop, directed by Shira Piven, in Los

Angeles, please come. I did. The workshop, a week in a small theater on Pico Boulevard, concluded with a single performance. Everyone we knew in Hollywood, or so it seemed, was crammed into that little theater for that performance. The play was terrible. Worse than it had ever been. We walked out of the theater and never said a single word to each other about it.

However, the biggest laugh in the play went in during that workshop. Contributed by an actor, the late Stephanie Mnookin: "When you start wearing Eileen Fisher, you might as well say, 'I give up.'" And one writer friend called afterward with a note. To my memory this is the only friend who called, but that is surely wrong as I have lovely, polite friends. His note was to fix the opening—make it clearer what the audience is in for, what the play is about. I thanked him and told him the play was d-e-a-d.

Time passes, I mean years—it's the summer of 2008—and a theater director, Karen Carpenter, calls. She had read the play long ago at the San Diego Old Globe, where it was vegetating. She had been lugging it around with her ever since. She had an opportunity to do a workshop and public performance/reading at the East Hampton Town Hall. Could she do our play? With Linda Lavin as Gingy, said Nora or Karen, depending on whom you asked. Linda Lavin agreed.

We implemented the note I'd received years before and not forgotten, probably because it rang true. It simply involved taking something at the end of the play and moving it to the beginning. I remember the afternoon we put the change in. We were working at my apartment, in the bedroom where my desk was. Nora had been sick now for two years, and collaborating was precious in a way that it hadn't been before. And just before or just after we did that note, Nora gave me a present, her enamel pansy ring, which I treasured.

The note helped the play, but mainly it was Linda Lavin. She was a brilliant Gingy.

There are many lessons in this. One: Never give up. We did. We shouldn't have. Thank you, Karen. Two: Sometimes the right actor makes all the difference. Three: Always be open to a note, and a subset of this, writers give great notes. Four: Luck can change when you least expect it.

Daryl Roth wanted to produce the play, and from then on everything went right and with great speed. Now I think of it as a perfect collaboration. The structure of the play, women's stories, gave Nora and me each breathing room. We rewrote our separate pieces and together we sharpened ensemble pieces. We worked together beautifully. It was truly about sisterhood: our own and the shared experiences of women. Every month we changed the cast and five new amazing actors performed it. Eventually 120 did it in New York City. I became friends with many of them.

Playwrights are respected, deeply respected. The intimacy and creativity of rehearsals, the excitement of women coming to see it was thrilling. The connection between the women onstage and the women in the audience was palpable. Personal.

Sometimes men came to see our play. We were happy to have them—they even laughed, but we never cared if they did. "Ninety-eight percent women tonight," our associate general manager, Jodi Carter, might report. Ninety-eight percent women. Fantastic.

What I loved most was that so many of our friends contributed. The play celebrates Heather's high heels, Amanda's wedding dress. That's Amanda who is Alice's daughter—Alice whom I went to high school with and who is still a close friend. It has Joy's black cigarette pants, Nancy's gang sweater, the underwire bra my friend Meredith gave to my friend Geralyn, Rosie's mother's bathrobe, Annie's paper dress, Gail's raincoat, Nora's purse, my lime-green winter coat.

Delia Ephron

The play is a patchwork of friendship, and friendship is collaboration, the best kind. The give-and-take of close friendship is collaboration on life.

. . . .

I dreamt about Nora last night. For the first time since she died. It made me happy because she was alive in the dream. A dream is a visit, a conjuring, the only way you might have a conversation with someone who has died and believe it is real. At least believe it while you're asleep (which may not be believing it).

Nora was on a single bed, not sick, just resting on a bed. We talked. I told her that I heard her new play was wonderful. I hadn't yet seen *Lucky Guy*. It was in pre-views. We were going to the opening together, the whole family. It was comforting to be able to tell her that *Lucky Guy* was wonderful. Her not being alive for it had been making me heartsick.

She said we should go right now and see "pieces of it."

That's an expression we always used about our own play. Over the two years it ran, we would stop by the the-ater and stay for a few pieces. And I would call her or she would call me and say, "I stayed for a few pieces," and give a report.

And then in the dream—the way, in a dream, one image is replaced by another—Nora was standing up now, wearing a party dress—a spectacular strapless taffeta party dress, gray (the prettiest bright gray), just the sort of dress a woman might remember every detail of and write about in the play we collaborated on, the play we colloquially referred to as *Love Loss*.

"We should go see pieces," she said to me in the dream.

And we did. We went off together.

Acknowledgments

I f it weren't for Trish Hall of the *New York Times*, I would never have begun this writing journey. My gratitude as well to Dorothy Rabinowitz of the *Wall Street Journal*. Deena Goldstone and Joy Horowitz—devoted friends and wonderful writers—read endlessly for me. I am in their debt. Also my thanks to Larry Mark, who is always generous with advice, now and over the years. A shout-out to all their dogs for undoubtedly raising their owners' spirits and sensitivities each day, and I have benefited from that: George, Simon, Bailey, Coral, Sadie, and Danny. My editor and publisher, David Rosenthal, does not have a dog. Otherwise he is perfect. I am blessed to have him. In fact, none of the amazing people at Blue

Acknowledgments

Rider Press have dogs, which is a mystery, but they are brilliant nevertheless: my editor, Sarah Hochman; Aileen Boyle; and Brian Ulicky. To my agents . . . I can never thank Lynn Nesbit enough—her support makes my writing life possible—and to Dorothy Vincent, my sincerest appreciation. Also to Joel Mason for being so generous with his talent, I owe you. Joel has two cats—Emma and Woody. Dorothy Vincent has two as well: Peter Washington Taub and Pedro Eugenio Borges Taub. While I don't totally get cats, I respect that others do.

The wisdom and heart of my husband, Jerome Kass, always guide me. And thank you, Honey, for inspiration. Right now she is probably where she isn't supposed to be, on the living room couch. My love to my sisters Hallie and Amy, and to the comforting memory of Nora.

About the Author

Delia Ephron is a bestselling author and screenwriter. Her movies include *The Sisterhood of the Traveling Pants*, *You've Got Mail*, *Hanging Up* (based on her novel), and *Michael*. She has written novels for adults and teenagers, including her most recent, *The Lion Is In*; books of humor, including *How to Eat Like a Child*; and essays. Her journalism has appeared in the *New York Times*, the *Wall Street Journal*, *O: The Oprah Magazine*, and *More*. Her hit play, *Love, Loss, and What I Wore* (cowritten with Nora Ephron), ran for more than two years Off-Broadway and has been performed all over the world, including in Paris, Rio, and Sydney. She lives in New York City.